Examining Doctoral Work

Written in clear, straight-forward language, *Examining Doctoral Work* considers how the practice of doctoral examination can be improved to ensure that both examiners and students can make the most of the assessment process.

This book analyses both good and bad practice to promote fair, thorough and productive examination. With insight into how to prepare for a viva, as well as a consideration of the responsibilities afterwards, the book de-mystifies this crucial part of the doctoral examination process to provide a comprehensive overview of the principles, criteria and processes needed to ensure success. Key points covered include:

- The different forms doctoral submission can take
- How examiners are chosen
- Where to begin when reading a thesis
- Managing your time as an examiner
- What makes a 'good' doctoral thesis?
- How to prepare for the viva
- How to develop a preliminary report
- The role of the supervisor before, during and after the viva
- Examiners' roles and responsibilities
- Working through agreements and disagreements
- Feeding back both orally and in writing.

Drawing from a mixture of personal experience, existing research and anecdote, this book is ideal reading for anyone new to the world of doctoral examination, or equally those looking to improve their practice.

Jerry Wellington was a Professor and Head of Research Degrees in the School of Education at the University of Sheffield, UK. He is now an educational consultant.

Key Guides for Effective Teaching in Higher Education Series
Edited by Kate Exley

This indispensable series is aimed at new lecturers, postgraduate students who have teaching time, Graduate Teaching Assistants, part-time tutors and demonstrators, as well as experienced teaching staff who may feel it's time to review their skills in teaching and learning.

Titles in this series will provide the teacher in higher education with practical, realistic guidance on the various different aspects of their teaching role, which is underpinned not only by current research in the field, but also by the extensive experience of individual authors, and with a keen eye kept on the limitations and opportunities therein. By bridging a gap between academic theory and practice, all titles will provide generic guidance on the topics covered, which is then brought to life through the use of short, illustrative examples drawn from a range of disciplines. All titles in the series will:

- represent up-to-date thinking and incorporate the use of computing and appropriate learning technology
- consider methods and approaches for teaching and learning when there is an increasing diversity in learning and a growth in student numbers
- encourage readers to reflect, critique and apply learning in their practice and professional context
- provide links and references to other work on the topic and research evidence where appropriate.

Titles in the series will prove invaluable whether they are used for self-study, as reference material when seeking teaching recognition or as part of a formal taught programme on teaching and learning in higher education (HE), and will also be of relevance to teaching staff working in further education (FE) settings.

Other titles in this series:

Giving a Lecture
From Presenting to Teaching, 2ed
Kate Exley and Reg Dennick
Using Technology to Support Learning and Teaching
Andy Fisher, Kate Exley and Dragos Ciobanu
Leading Learning and Teaching in Higher Education
The Key Guide to Designing and Delivering Courses
Doug Parkin

Small Group Teaching
Seminars, Tutorials and Workshops, 2ed
Kate Exley, Reg Dennick and Andrew Fisher
Developing Your Teaching
Towards Excellence, 2ed
Peter Kahn and Lorraine Anderson
Designing Learning From Module Outline to Effective Teaching, 2ed
Christopher Butcher, Clara Davies and Melissa Highton

For more information about this series, please visit: https://www.routledge.com/Key-Guides-for-Effective-Teaching-in-Higher-Education/book-series/SE0746

Examining Doctoral Work
Exploring Principles, Criteria and Processes

Jerry Wellington

LONDON AND NEW YORK

First published 2021
by Routledge
2 Park Square, Milton Park, Abingdon, Oxon OX14 4RN

and by Routledge
52 Vanderbilt Avenue, New York, NY 10017

Routledge is an imprint of the Taylor & Francis Group, an informa business

© 2021 Jerry Wellington

The right of Jerry Wellington to be identified as author of this
work has been asserted by him in accordance with sections 77 and
78 of the Copyright, Designs and Patents Act 1988.

All rights reserved. No part of this book may be reprinted
or reproduced or utilised in any form or by any electronic,
mechanical, or other means, now known or hereafter invented,
including photocopying and recording, or in any information
storage or retrieval system, without permission in writing from
the publishers.

Trademark notice: Product or corporate names may be trademarks
or registered trademarks, and are used only for identification and
explanation without intent to infringe.

British Library Cataloguing-in-Publication Data
A catalogue record for this book is available from the British Library

Library of Congress Cataloging-in-Publication Data
Names: Wellington, J. J. (Jerry J.), author.
Title: Examining doctoral work : exploring principles, criteria and
    processes / Jerry Wellington.
Description: New York, NY : Routledge, 2021. | Series: Key guides for
    effective teaching in higher education | Includes bibliographical
    references and index.
Identifiers: LCCN 2020014782 (print) | LCCN 2020014783 (ebook) |
    ISBN 9780367431594 (hardback) | ISBN 9780367431600
    (paperback) | ISBN 9781003001607 (ebook)
Subjects: LCSH: Doctor of philosophy degree. | Oral examinations.
    Classification: LCC LB2386 .W45 2021 (print) | LCC LB2386 (ebook) |
    DDC 378.2/42—dc23
LC record available at https://lccn.loc.gov/2020014782
LC ebook record available at https://lccn.loc.gov/2020014783

ISBN: 978-0-367-43159-4 (hbk)
ISBN: 978-0-367-43160-0 (pbk)
ISBN: 978-1-003-00160-7 (ebk)

Typeset in Perpetua
by Swales & Willis, Exeter, Devon, UK

Contents

Series editor introduction	vi
Preface	ix

PART I
Exploring the meaning of doctorateness   **1**

1	A brave new world of doctorates?	3
2	What is a doctorate?	18
3	Enacting 'doctorateness': doctoral examining in practice	30

PART II
Practical aspects of the doctoral examining process   **39**

4	Who are the examiners and what do they look for?	41
5	Preparing the preliminary, independent reports	51

PART III
Judgements, decisions and their aftermath   **61**

6	Making the decision	63
7	The oral examination (live voice): why, what and how	71
8	Post examination: the examiners' and Chair's roles and responsibilities	91

References	101
Index	105

Series editor introduction

THE SERIES

The Key Guides for Effective Teaching in Higher Education were initially discussed as an idea in 2002, and the first group of four titles were published in 2004. New titles have continued to be added and the Series now boasts twelve books (with new titles and further new editions of some of the older volumes in the pipeline).

It has always been intended that the books would be primarily of use to new teachers in universities and colleges. It has been exciting to see them being used to support postgraduate certificate programmes in teaching and learning for new academic staff and clinical teachers, and also the skills training programmes for post-graduate students who are beginning to teach. A less anticipated, but very valued, readership has been the experienced teachers who have dipped into the books when reviewing their teaching or referenced them when making claims for teaching recognition or promotion. Authors are very grateful to these colleagues who have given constructive feedback and made further suggestions on teaching approaches and shared examples of their practice, all of which has fed forward into later editions of titles.

In the UK, the work of the Higher Education Academy (HEA), now part of Advance HE, in developing a Professional Standard Framework (UKPSF), on behalf of the sector, has also raised the importance of providing good quality guidance and support for those beginning their teaching careers. It is therefore intended that the series would also provide a useful set of sources for those seeking to gain professional recognition for their practice against the UKPSF.

KEY THEMES OF THE SERIES

The books are all attempting to combine two things: to be very practical and provide lots of examples of methods and techniques, and also to link to educational theory and underpinning research. Articles are referenced, further readings are suggested and researchers in the field are quoted. There is also much enthusiasm here to link to the wide range of teaching development activities thriving in the disciplines, supported by the small grant schemes and conferences provided by Advance HE, Society for Research in Higher Education, Professional bodies etc. The need to tailor teaching approaches to meet the demands of different subject areas and to provide new teachers with examples of practice that are easily recognisable in their fields of study is seen as being very important by all the series authors. To this end the books include many examples drawn from a wide range of academic subjects and different kinds of Higher Education institutions. This theme of diversity is also embraced when considering the heterogeneous groups of students we now teach and the colleagues we work alongside. Students and teachers alike include people of different age, experience, knowledge, skills, culture, language, etc., and all the books include discussion of the issues and demands this places on teachers and learners in today's universities.

In the series as a whole there is also more than half an eye trying to peer into the future – what will teaching and learning look like in 10 or 20 years' time? How will student expectations, government policy, funding streams, and new technological advances and legislation affect what happens in our learning spaces of the future? What impact will this have on the way teaching is led and managed in institutions. You will see, therefore, that many of the books do include chapters that aim to look ahead and tap into the thinking of our most innovative and creative teachers and teaching leaders in an attempt to crystal-ball gaze. So these were the original ideas underpinning the series, and my co-authors and I have tried hard to keep them in mind as we researched our topics and typed away. We really hope that you find the books to be useful and interesting, whether you are a new teacher just starting out in your teaching career, or you are an experienced teacher reflecting on your practice and reviewing what you do.

EXAMINING DOCTORAL WORK: EXPLORING PRINCIPLES, CRITERIA AND PROCESSES

Jerry has done a super job in pulling together a coherent and very readable volume giving clear guidance on the examination of doctoral candidates. His personal experience shines through the pages but he also draws upon a wider

SERIES EDITOR INTRODUCTION

exploration of current policies, procedures and practices from across the UK and beyond. The doctorate has changed significantly in the last 20 years and yet at its heart, it remains a unique challenge in independent research and critical thinking. Jerry considers the implications of this 'brave new world' for students, supervisors, institutions but centrally, for internal and external examiners. Taking the reader, step-by-step through the assessment process, he clarifies the roles and responsibilities of all involved. This is a very practical book which provides so many useful nuggets of information, advice and honestly honed insights – I am sure a new examiner will find it absolutely invaluable but also, experienced examiners will find much to relate to and use to reflect upon their own experiences and practice.

Kate Exley
Series Editor

Preface

Why do I think that there is a need for this book? There are already many useful articles and books on the doctoral examination process and the viva and these are shown in a comprehensive list of Further Reading at the end of each chapter. This book sets out to explore the whole process in its current context under one cover, whilst being as honest, brief and direct as possible. In places it uses a mixture of personal experience and anecdote but the book also draws upon and references the extensive literature that has been published on doctoral examining over recent decades. The book is aimed primarily at new staff who are teaching and examining in higher education, although I have written it so that it will also be valuable to supervisors and students by de-mystifying the entire doctoral examination process.

Later chapters in the book, on the practice of examining, relate largely to UK procedures and practices (involving the oral examination or viva voce) and these are also followed in several other countries. However, the bulk of the book's content focuses on doctoral examination principles, criteria and processes which are practiced worldwide.

There is (in my view) a scarcity of staff development which is aimed at producing civilised, thorough and fair doctoral examiners (both internal and external). I have provided many staff development workshops around the UK and elsewhere (e.g. South Africa and Canada) on doctoral examining and my perception is that 'courses' on this area are not widespread in universities. New staff are often expected to 'just do it' and their fall-back position is sometimes 'do unto others as was done to me' – not a good basis for maintaining either fairness or high doctoral standards.

The book should remain valuable as long as the doctorate is examined in the current way, i.e. by a submission of some kind (usually a written

PREFACE

dissertation) followed by an oral examination involving at least one external examiner. I would suggest that this practice will continue for the foreseeable future.

THE CURRENT CONTEXT TO THIS BOOK

In some ways, the doctorate has changed enormously over the forty years in which I have worked in higher education. I will discuss this early in the book. Changes such as the rise in professional doctorates, the increased scrutiny of supervision, the necessity to keep records (rightly in my view) and the steady growth in numbers have all changed the context for the examination process. However, in some ways, the actual assessment process has not changed greatly. A person observing a viva voce (not that they would be allowed to – a contentious point) in 1982 (when I did my first viva) would see a largely similar set-up to an observer in 2020. The seating arrangement, the room layout and the people sitting in it would be the same except perhaps for the presence of an 'independent chair', now widely used in universities.

My task in this book is to discuss the changes that are relevant alongside the features that have remained the same. I will examine good and bad practice both now and over recent years. The examination of the doctorate is a unique form of assessment in terms of the process and the people involved. It is a key, memorable event in the lives of the students and it is therefore the duty of those involved to make it as thorough, fair, robust and productive as possible. I see it as a formative process (rather than solely summative) in that an excellent doctoral examination can be the launching point for a student's publications and future career.

Part I

Exploring the meaning of doctorateness

Chapter 1

A brave new world of doctorates?

THE CHANGING CONTEXT FOR THE DOCTORATE AND ITS INFLUENCE ON EXAMINING

When I started supervising in the 1980s it was (I am sorry to say) a fairly laid back affair. It was usually one-to-one (co-supervision was not common let alone compulsory). I did make regular appointments with the student and although our meetings were enjoyable and challenging for both parties they rarely had a mutually agreed agenda and notes were not taken, still less stored and looked back on. This was bad practice; this chapter reflects on the huge improvements that have been made in doctoral education.

The main change, in two nutshells, has been from professional self-regulation to evidence-based quality control, and, at the same time, from a loose autonomy to a tight accountability.

These changes have had both positive and negative impacts. To begin with the positive, the supervision process is no longer as hidden as it once was. Co-supervision, for example, has opened up the process and has often led to improved guidance and stimulation for the student. From supervisors being left alone to 'just get on with it', and conduct supervision behind closed doors in their own unique (perhaps idiosyncratic fashion), the move towards greater transparency has at least led to the sharing of good practice. This has been enhanced by a growth (though not universal) in supervisor 'training', or more accurately 'development', in universities. Another impact of quality control and accountability has been the pressure on students and supervisors to achieve timely submission. A few decades ago I met a PhD student on a research 'training' course who told me she had been working on her doctorate for 12 years.

3

I asked her why. She said: 'because I am enjoying it and don't want it to end'. (Incidentally, and importantly, she was self-funded!) I cannot imagine that happening now. Time pressures have led to more submissions being on time and a reduction in the 'risk' those students might take with their work. Many students have said to me that they 'just want to get it done'. Completion rates may have improved, but opponents of quality control and time keeping will argue that this has reduced risk taking, stifled originality and led to 'managed mediocrity'. An article entitled 'It's a PhD not a Nobel Prize' published in 2002 neatly captures this change (Mullins and Kiley 2002). A PhD is no longer someone's 'life's work' as perhaps it was once viewed. Equally, time pressures, or the clock ticking on scholarships, may lead to early submissions before a doctorate is fully ready, as in: 'Let's give it a go, submit now and see what happens. We will at least get feedback from the examiners ...'. I have also heard, from more than one supervisor, the football analogy of 'Let's get it submitted and go for a 1–0 victory'.

Another change that came about early this century resulted from the Roberts Review, which we discuss later. Sir Gareth Roberts, who was vice chancellor at the University of Sheffield when I was a young professor there, instigated a move towards the development of 'generic, transferable skills' as part of the doctoral programme. For many this had clear advantages for the students, and it was largely seen as an improvement in their 'employability'. But for others the pressure to develop generic skills – and to have this development audited – was an unwanted diversion from 'real research' and original inquiry.

Many of the changes are seen as a key feature in the growth of what has now become known as the 'audit culture'. For example, an increasing number of questions have been asked about the *impact of the doctorate*. This has arisen from the growth in concern (even consternation perhaps) in higher education and amongst wider stakeholders, such as industry, with the value, outcomes, performance and returns on public investment arising from doctoral work.

To cut a long discussion short, I have summarised in Table 1.1, in a polarised fashion, the opposing views that have been expressed on the increasing moves towards regulation of the doctorate.

In parallel with the above shifts in doctoral education another radical change has taken place which has had a major impact on doctoral examining: the growth of diversity. As the context has changed so has the tendency towards diversity in doctorates.

4

A BRAVE NEW WORLD OF DOCTORATES?

TABLE 1.1 Regulatory contexts: have they led to standardisation or improvement? Two polarised viewpoints

POSITIVE – FOR REGULATION	NEGATIVE
A timely end to a laissez-faire, behind closed doors approach	Severe scrutiny, constant audit
Demise of the secret garden	Removed autonomy, stifled originality
Wise risk management	An end to risk, managed mediocrity
Pragmatism, improved completion rates, emphasis on making the doctorate 'do-able'	Constant time keeping, closed-ended, excessive/unhelpful pressure to complete
End of unwanted risk taking	Doctorates by numbers
Supervisor training improves completion rates	Supervisors cannot be trained – supervisor development is the aim (reflective practice)
Introduction of generic skills agenda to increase, for example, employability	Skills demand reduces completion rates (it gets in the way of the doctoral contribution)
Careful time keeping – which may help with timely submission	Time pressures can bring undue stress and either 'ordinary/just good enough' or early submissions
Increased scrutiny of doctoral assessment	Reduced autonomy of doctoral examiners
Longer and more explicit written regulations on the criteria for a doctorate and the conduct of examinations	Examiners no longer allowed to 'just get on with it'

DOCTORAL DIVERSITY

Quite simply, doctorates are far more diverse than they were even 10 years ago and certainly vastly different to doctoral provision in (say) the 1980s and 1990s. This has huge implications for the examination of doctoral work and for the notion of 'doctorateness' which is discussed in detail later.

5

Diversity can be viewed as having three dimensions or contexts, rather like concentric circles. First, at the micro level, there is now greater diversity in doctoral programmes and the students they attract. The programmes offered and the doctoral teaching 'delivered' (a word I detest) are more varied then ever – teaching or pedagogy, has moved from being largely one-to-one (or one-to-two in co-supervision) to a more distributed form of pedagogy (see next section). Consequently, assessment en route to the final award has changed from being one final event (often the viva – see later) to continuous assessment at different phases of the 'doctoral journey' (a hackneyed metaphor but the most common!). Programmes are now structured so that feedback and assessment occurs at various 'milestones' (another metaphor, sorry). Formative feedback or assessment may occur in a 'research training' phase, in the nurturing of a portfolio or in the development of so-called generic skills. Progressive assessment is particularly true of professional doctorates (PDs/Prof Docs) where, for example, a 'taught' first part is assessed before students can proceed to the second part, the dissertation phase.

To sum up this first level of diversity, the benefits to students are immense: they have greater choice of doctoral routes, access is more open, assessment may be less final or brutal, provision is more flexible, and thus participation is so much wider. Programmes can be matched to students' varying needs, lifestyles, family situations, ages and learning styles.

The second aspect of diversity is at institutional level (the mesa level). Briefly, we can say that far more universities are involved in doctoral work; the type, size, reputation, values, ethos, culture and structure of institutions offering doctoral programmes have diverged enormously as a result. For the university, diversity has widened the potential pool of students. Each higher education institution (HEI) can choose its own style of provision and target audience. Thus HEIs have become more responsive to outside needs in four areas: students, employers, society and professions.

Finally, at the macro level, the society in which doctoral work is occurring has changed in terms of graduate opportunities, the nature and range of employment, the demand for doctorates by employers and the professions, and the post-doctoral impact of successful students in those areas. In particular, the nature and attitude of the professions which give rise to the appetite for their staff to seek doctorates and then subsequently the demand for them, has changed steadily and is one of the factors behind the rise in professional doctorates.

In summary, the three dimensions of the growth in diversity of doctorates have had a huge impact. To take an ecological line, we now experience

A BRAVE NEW WORLD OF DOCTORATES?

▨ TABLE 1.2 List of possible doctoral titles (from University of Leicester handbook)

Doctor of Philosophy (PhD)

Doctor of Psychology (PsyD)

Doctor of Medicine (MD)

Doctor of Clinical Psychology (DClinPsy)

Doctor of Social Sciences (DSocSci)

Doctor of Education (EdD)

Doctor of Engineering (EngD)

greater variation, competition, adaptation, survival of the fittest and natural selection, sometimes leading to extinction when an institution abandons one or more of its doctoral programmes. For students, it has been, and still is, a question of finding their niche or favoured habitat. Table 1.2 shows some of the titles of doctorates now available in one university in the UK.

In the USA, to take another example, there is also the DNP (Doctor of Nursing Practice, with over 100 programmes), PharmD (Doctor of Pharmacy), Doctor of Law, and the DPT (Doctor of Physical Therapy).

Routes, types of doctorate and modes of submission

We have also witnessed an increase in the 'types of doctorate' now available, principally among PhDs. There has been the 'new route' PhD, often called the integrated PhD, and also the 'PhD by publication'. The new route/integrated PhD involves (for full time students) starting with a one year Masters' degree followed by the expected three years to complete the PhD dissertation ready for submission. This is then assessed in the usual way, explained fully later.

The 'PhD by publication' as a mode of submission has been ideal for the academic who has built up a list of published work in their chosen field but has never had either the time or the inclination to create a single document in the form of a traditional dissertation. The candidate then submits a portfolio of work they have published. This may be in the form of a peer-reviewed book, or book chapters together with an ongoing series of refereed articles in acceptable journals. A covering statement must show the coherence and the 'driving force' behind the portfolio; as well as explaining how the portfolio is a coherent body of work, the candidate must also make explicit the 'original contribution' that their work has made. This vitally important statement is then submitted alongside the publications themselves. This entire submission will be sent to both or all the examiners and the assessment will proceed using the criteria and the procedures described in later chapters. In my experience, this makes for an excellent viva voce! The student may typically be a 'mid-career academic' and the whole procedure offers them the challenging task of reflecting on their work thus far and the contribution they have made: not an easy task.

A useful summary of 'four routes' to the doctorate is given at:

www.prospects.ac.uk/postgraduate-study/phd-study/4-routes-to-getting-a-doctorate

Increased diversity has also had a major impact on the practice of doctoral assessment and the behaviour of examiners, as we see later.

DRAWBACKS AND CHALLENGES IN DIVERSITY

Diversity has brought many advantages and widely increased opportunities for students and institutions. But every silver lining has a cloud. Education systems seem to have a peculiar talent for converting a seemingly 'horizontal' diversity into a 'vertical' hierarchy. This has happened throughout the history of new qualifications being introduced into education at the 16 to 18 phase and into Higher Education. The phenomenon was neatly summed up by Raymond Bourdon in 1974 when he wrote of patterns of inequality:

> In highly structured societies, the greater the variety of different routes through the system, the greater the likelihood that the education system will reproduce or intensify the existing pattern of inequalities.
>
> (Bourdon 1974)

It seems that some doctorates are perceived as being more equal than others. This was certainly the case with the PhD versus the professional doctorate in its early stages. In the 1990s I once assessed, as internal examiner, an excellent professional doctorate thesis with an external examiner from a top ranked university who was not familiar with the processes or structure of a Prof Doc (despite my trying to explain them to him). After a successful viva at which the student passed with minor corrections he said to her: 'With a bit more work you could make this into a PhD.' My reaction and hers were not favourable. Parity of esteem, or absence of it, is a resilient perception.

The numbers and the variety of students pursuing doctorates have grown considerably. Another outcome of diversity has brought the welcome addition of diverse 'forms' of doctoral submission, e.g. the traditional PhD dissertation, shorter theses for Prof Docs, doctorates via publication, and so on. This implies new, often exciting, challenges for examiners. Universities have tried to maintain criteria and standards by which 'doctorateness' can be judged but it could be argued that the concept itself has become more elusive and less definable as diversity has grown. We look at this in later chapters.

FROM PRIVATE TO PUBLIC: 'DISTRIBUTED PEDAGOGY' IN DOCTORAL EDUCATION

As doctoral pedagogy has changed and we move from one-to-one (or -two) models of supervision towards a broader view of when and where doctoral education takes place we see the importance of networks of learning in which students take the active role, i.e. they are no longer passive recipients of supervision. They will learn from a wider, more distributed range of people and sources. We need to consider:

- The cohort effect
- Peer learning, e.g. critical friends, student-led seminars
- Peer support
- Conference presentations
- Families and friends
- Employers (especially Prof Docs)
- University mentors
- Existing student mentors/buddies
- 'Doctoral development' programmes, workshops
- Internet links, websites, social media
- Relationships/links with other staff, staff seminars
- Research environments (attachment to projects, research centres).

Thus in recent decades, there has been a move from a focus on 'private' supervision and a stress on independence and autonomy to one of networking, socially situated learning and collaboration. Doctoral students, especially on professional doctorate programmes, will form a 'cohort' or a group which is moving towards the final examination together; this cohort can have a huge positive effect on not only the student's progress and learning experiences but also on their motivation, i.e. the affective aspect of their doctorate as well as the cognitive. Doctoral students will meet, listen to and learn from a far wider range of people than was the case when supervision was behind closed doors between consenting adults. What is the relevance of these changes for doctoral assessment and examination?

We cannot consider every consequence of these changes but one immediate point springs to mind: over the full period of their 'journey', doctoral students will be asked far more questions about their work, at much more frequent intervals and by a far wider range of people. They will be asked questions by their peers and critical friends, by people they present to at conferences, and by university staff other than their supervisor(s). In many ways, therefore, they will be better prepared for their dissertation submission and certainly more able to succeed in the intense questioning about their work that is the viva voce.

DOES THE PROFESSIONAL DOCTORATE DIFFER FROM A PHD? IF SO, HOW?

Professional doctorates have been established for over three decades now: in management, engineering, the built environment, education, nursing, law and other fields of scholarship. Yet the question posed above is still asked. I first examined a professional doctorate in the 1990s when there was a certain amount of scepticism bordering on cynicism toward the 'Prof Doc'. It was accused of, or labelled as, a 'taught' doctorate; it was described as a doctorate for researching professionals rather than professional researchers. There were even accusations of 'dumbing down' and complaints that the doctorate would become more accessible and widespread – no longer for the elite – as if this were a bad thing. The issue of parity of esteem between the traditional PhD (not that the PhD really exists now in its original form) and the Prof Doc still lingers on in my experience.

Another issue arose: the push to make doctorates more connected to the economy, industry, employers and the professions. Incidentally, this occurred not only with the professional doctorate but with initiatives in the PhD student's programme which introduced generic and transferable skills as well as a 'training' element in some form. But the Prof Doc was said by some to concern a different category of knowledge to the traditional PhD.

TABLE 1.3 Modes of knowledge (the extremes)

ACADEMIC	VOCATIONAL
Pure	Messy
Theoretical	Practical
Disembedded	Embedded
Universalisable	Situational
Independent of context	Context dependent
Off the job	On the job
Abstract	Concrete
'Academic knowledge'; knowledge that/why	Knowledge how; knowledge in action
Conceptual	Procedural

Talk, and writing, arose about modes of knowledge. I cannot explore this in detail here but in brief a division was presented between academic and vocational knowledge – I have summed this up (without doing it justice) in a very simplistic table (see Table 1.3).

Of course, this table is a gross over simplification of the useful distinctions that have been put forward in contemplating the nature of knowledge (the business of epistemology). But as I said earlier, systems seem to possess the knack of turning diversity into a hierarchy and this has been true with the distinction between academic knowledge and vocational (at all levels of education in fact).

In reality, and certainly in my own experience of supervising and examining, there are many PhDs which veer towards the right side of the above table (for example by having valuable practical implications) and many Prof Docs which generate knowledge nearer the left side, e.g. by contributing to theory or having a heavy conceptual content.

We need to be extremely careful in the current context when we consider categories of doctorate – for there are important practical differences for doctoral work depending on whether and how we consider that a Prof Doc differs from a PhD.

a. No difference: if there is no difference then they would require similar styles of supervision but more importantly the examination process for both types of doctorate should be the same as should the criteria (both written and tacit) for the award of the degree. The choice of examiners (discussed in Chapter 4) should also be made using the same criteria. For example, the idea of bringing people in as examiners from employment or industry for the Prof Doc would hardly seem relevant if there is no difference.

b. On the other hand, if the PhD is truly of a different nature when compared with a Prof Doc, then perhaps the supervision process should differ, the entire examination process including examiner choice and those present for a viva should be different, different documentation and criteria for 'doctorateness' (see later) should be written down and even the key question of what counts as a 'contribution' would vary from one award to another (again discussed later).

Convergence or divergence?

We cannot discuss this fully here but there has been considerable discussion about whether the PhD and the professional doctorate have actually converged over recent decades (see for example Hoddell et al. 2002). This has occurred due to several factors: first, the growth of the PD alongside changes in the PhD with the introduction of an RTP (research training programme) or a DDP (doctoral development programme) and some years ago with the so-called 'new route PhD'. Second, the two types of doctorate have had a mutual influence on each other – not least because the same staff in universities are often teaching on and supervising students from both routes at the same time. Equally, examiners such as myself who started by examining only the traditional PhD have examined dissertations in both categories of doctorate, internally and externally.

EXAMINING IN THE UK AND OTHER COUNTRIES AND HOW 'SYSTEMS' VARY AROUND THE WORLD

We do not have the space here to make a full comparative study of doctoral education around the world but there is an extensive literature on this which shows that many of the trends in the English-speaking countries mentioned already have occurred worldwide. Two useful articles which take a global perspective are discussed below:

1. Andres, I, S Bengtsen, Liliana del Pilar Gallego Castano, Barbara Crossouard, Jeffrey M. Keefer and Kirsi Pyhalto (2015) Drivers and Interpretations of Doctoral Education Today: National Comparisons, *Frontline Learning Research* Vol.3 No. 3 Special Issue 5–22 ISSN 2295–3159 http://dx.doi.org/10.14786/flr.v3i3.177

   They compare recent changes in each of the following countries: Canada, Colombia, Denmark, Finland, the UK and the USA. They contend that there are three 'global drivers' in doctoral education worldwide: massification of doctoral education, professionalisation of doctoral education and careers, and the development of various quality assurance systems.

2. Glasgow, M and H Dreher (2011) Global Perspectives on the Professional Doctorate, *International Journal of Nursing Studies* 48 403–408. Glasgow and Dreher look at the contrast between the PD and the PhD. They argue that the researching professional should be the leader in generating practice-based evidence leading to practice knowledge. They contrast this mode of knowledge with the 'professional researcher' who 'should produce knowledge that is more theoretical or generate more evidence-based practice knowledge when working with larger data sets with an emphasis on heterogeneity of samples and the generalizability of findings'.

Personally, I am not convinced, from my own experience, that this distinction is watertight. I have supervised PhDs which have not used large data sets with heterogeneous samples – nor have the findings always been generalisable. Equally, I have examined and supervised numerous PDs which have not always led to so-called 'practice knowledge'. For example, they may have been more concerned with policy and in fact some PDs do use large data sets for examining policy and practice.

Interestingly, they point out that it is often staff who have PhDs themselves 'who become the curriculum architects of various PD programmes. It is therefore not surprising that there is 'murkiness in doctoral curricula praxis when future researching professionals are exclusively taught and mentored by professional researchers' (p.403). They ask if the PD is 'equal but different'. Both these points have implications for doctoral assessment as we will see later. Many assessors of PDs will have come through the traditional

PhD route and I argue later that the issue of parity of esteem, whereby all doctorates are equal but some are more equal than others, is still lingering.

Finally, the website below reports a study of PhD programmes around the world:

https://phys.org/news/2017-09-phd-countries.html
accessed 28/01/2020

AND FINALLY ... WHAT CAN EXAMINERS GAIN FROM BECOMING INVOLVED?

There is surprisingly little literature on this but the question is well worth considering in this introductory chapter: what's in it for us, the examiners? Well, it certainly involves a lot of time and mental effort: reading the dissertation, making notes on it, sending in a preliminary report, attending and conducting a viva voce (in most cases), conferring with other examiners and sometimes a chair, writing a final report and then in many cases checking at a later date to see if corrections have been made or (more work still) assessing a re-submission. I always find it hard to estimate the time it takes me to examine a doctorate but I would guess it is in the region of 30 to 40 hours of work (though I may be very slow!).

So what are the plus sides? Well, certainly we owe it to colleagues and to students who may be future members of academia or contributors to the economy to be collegial and to do our duty. So for me the community or collegiality aspect of examining is foremost. But wearing a more utilitarian hat, the process of examining a doctorate has many tangible benefits. First, it enhances our connections and our networks, i.e. our social and academic capital. By examining we meet new people: certainly the student, but often fellow academics who are involved in the exam process. These meetings and links can be valuable not only at the time but often in the future, e.g. for collaboration, finding people who may make good examiners for our own students, for research connections and so on.

Second, I always find that by examining a doctorate I learn something. It may be a case of discovering new and unexpected literature – one of the criteria for judging a doctorate (see later) is that its review of the literature contains some new and unexpected reading – not just the usual suspects. Many theses are highly stimulating. The literature they explore may make you want to go away and read something new, especially when the student has engaged in lateral thinking during their literature review. The findings, conclusions and 'contribution' (see later) can also be highly stimulating:

sometimes changing your own thinking and values. One can also learn from the way a thesis is written, structured and presented. Many follow a traditional pattern (which is fine) but others present either literature or discussion or findings in an unusual way (sometimes more successfully than others).

Connected with this second point is the real privilege of reading or hearing new ideas and insights presented by students in either the written form or in the 'heat' of the viva voce.

A third benefit in examining is that it can and will improve one's own supervision. One can learn by seeing top quality supervision and student support in action; on the negative side, one may also glean some insight into 'how not to do it'. Equally, the experience of examining alongside one other person or more enables one to learn from them and the way they evaluate and assess doctoral work. Thus, the learning process will improve one's own ability as an examiner as well as a supervisor.

Finally, the experience of examining at doctoral level is a promotion criterion in some cases and even if not an explicit criterion in your own university it can certainly be an asset to a CV.

To summarise, acting as either internal or external examiner for a doctoral dissertation involves both time and hard work but can be enjoyable, collegial and rewarding. It has both intrinsic and extrinsic benefits.

IN SUMMARY

The doctorate has changed. Factors effecting this change have been: the demand of doctorates to connect with the economy, industry, employers and the professions; the rise of the 'audit culture' bringing about time pressures to complete and transparency in supervision and assessment; the demand for 'flexible delivery' which can include blended learning (a mix of on-line and face-to-face learning) or solely on-line provision, in turn linked to a huge rise in student numbers engaging in doctoral work; a consequent growth in the numbers of HE staff who must now engage with supervision and doctoral assessment; the emphasis on generic, transferable skills as an explicit feature of the doctorate; and the huge growth of the professional doctorate.

These changes have been, in my personal view, changes for the better. However, critics of the evolution of the doctorate have spoken or written of: the 'dumbing down' of the doctorate; the lure of the 'Doctor' title in career enhancement as the main motivator, rather than the pursuit of knowledge for its own sake; and the loss of freedom and flair of supervisors and examiners as accountability has taken over from autonomy.

The changes outlined in this chapter have had a large influence on the doctoral examining process; and yet in many ways the nature of the doctorate and the assessment of 'doctorateness' have remained constant, as we discuss in the next chapter.

 FURTHER READING

On the diversity of doctorates and their evolution see:

Bourner, T., R. Bowden, and S. Laing. 1999. A National Profile of Research Degree Awards: Innovation, Clarity and Coherence. *Higher Education Quarterly* 53 (3): 264–280.

Green, H., and S. Powell. 2005. *Doctoral study in contemporary higher education*. Buckingham: Open University Press.

Hoddell, S., D. Street, and H. Wildblood. 2002. Doctorates – Converging or Diverging Patterns of Provision. *Quality Assurance in Education* 10 (2): 61–70.

Laing, S., and T. Brabazon. 2007. Creative Doctorates, Creative Education? Aligning Universities with the Creative Economy. *Nebula* 4 (2): 253.

Lester, S. 2004. Conceptualising the Practitioner Doctorate. *Studies in Higher Education* 29 (6): 757.

Noble, K. A. 1994. *Changing doctoral degrees: An international perspective*. Buckingham: Society for Research into Higher Education and Open University Press.

Park, C. 2005. New Variant PhD: The Changing Nature of the Doctorate in the UK. *Journal of Higher Education Policy and Management* 27 (2): 189–207.

Simpson, R. 1983. *How the PhD came to Britain*. Guildford: Society for Research into Higher Education.

Usher, R. 2002. A Diversity of Doctorates: Fitness for the Knowledge Economy? *Higher Education Research and Development* 21 (2): 143–153.

On the nature and range of professional doctorates now on offer in the UK and worldwide see:

Bourner, T., R. Bowden, and S. Laing. 2001. Professional Doctorates in England. *Studies in Higher Education* 26 (1): 65–83.

Bourner, T., R. Bowden, and S. Laing. 2002. Professional Doctorates in the UK and Australia: Not a World of Difference. *Higher Education Review* 35 (1): 76–87.

Brown, K., and C. Cooke. 2010. *Professional doctorate awards in the UK*. Staffordshire: UK Council for Graduate Education.

Chiteng Kot, F., and D. Hendel. 2011. Emergence and Growth of Professional Doctorates in the United States, United Kingdom, Canada and Australia: A Comparative Analysis. *Studies in Higher Education* 37 (3): 1–20.

Fink, D. 2006. The Professional Doctorate: Its Relativity to the Ph.D. and Relevance for the Knowledge Economy. *International Journal of Doctoral Studies* 3: 35–44.

Maxwell, T. W. 2011. Australian Professional Doctorates: Mapping, Distinctiveness, Stress and Prospects. *Work Based Learning e-Journal* 2 (1): 24.

Neumann, R. 2005. Doctoral Differences: Professional Doctorates and PhDs Compared. *Journal of Higher Education Policy and Management* 27 (2): 173–188.

Maxwell, T. 2003. From First to Second Generation Professional Doctorates. *Studies in Higher Education* 28 (3): 27.

Scott, D., A. Brown, I. Lunt, and L. Thorne. 2004. *Professional doctorates: Integrating professional and academic knowledge.* Maidenhead: Open University Press.

For a discussion of practice based doctorates and the issues they raise for assessment see:

Winter, R., M. Griffiths, and K. Green. 2000. The "Academic" Qualities of Practice: What are the Criteria for a Practice-based PhD?. *Studies in Higher Education* 25: 25–37.

And finally: metaphors abound in the discussion of doctoral journeys, supervision and assessment. For a classic discussion of how we cannot get by without them see:

Lakoff, G., and M. Johnson. 1980. *Metaphors we live by.* Chicago: University of Chicago Press.

WEBSITES

On the varying types of doctorate in the UK see both sites below:

www.vitae.ac.uk/doing-research/are-you-thinking-of-doing-a-phd/what-is-a-doctorate-1/common-types-of-doctoral-programme-in-the-uk

www.prospects.ac.uk/postgraduate-study/phd-study/4-routes-to-getting-a-doctorate

Vitae also provide a useful summary of doctoral programmes in the UK:

www.vitae.ac.uk/doing-research/are-you-thinking-of-doing-a-phd/what-is-a-doctorate-1/common-types-of-doctoral-programme-in-the-uk

This site, 'Find a PhD', gives information on other doctorates across the world:

www.findaphd.com/advice/finding/

Chapter 2

What is a doctorate?

'DOCTORATENESS' – CAN WE MAKE THIS EXPLICIT?

It is the biggest question posed in this book and it is one that must continually be asked as the doctorate and its context evolve. The issue of 'doctorateness' is a recurring debate which needs to be kept alive and revisited regularly (Gallie 1956). In Chapters 2 and 3, I suggest six different areas or arenas in which the question can be addressed, forming a framework which can be used for assessment. Having looked at each area, I suggest that we should not be seeking some essential meaning of the term but that we should look for 'family resemblances' across the wide range of doctorates now available to search for a better understanding of the nature of doctorateness and thereby improve the whole assessment process.

VARIATION AND EVOLUTION

There has always been something dynamic and evolving about the doctorate and its nature. This has occurred across time, from the early medieval idea of a 'licence to teach' through to its more Humboldtian conception as a research degree in Germany, and now to the current era of auditing, accountability, quality assurance and regulation (Quality Assurance Agency 2004; Simpson 1983; Taylor and Beasley 2005; Wellington 2010a). The doctorate can also be seen in different forms across the world (Green and Powell 2005; Powell and Green 2007). In short, the notion of a doctorate varies across space, time and different disciplines.

We have seen that in the current context, the doctorate is characterised more by diversity than uniformity (Neumann 2003, 2007; Usher 2002). As Park (2005) put it some time ago, we now have the 'new variant PhD'; and

18

this lies alongside the wide range of professional and practice based doctorates now available. Thus variability, across countries and disciplines, is a key factor when we seek to understand the doctorate.

WHY BOTHER WITH THE QUESTION?

Is the discussion of the question of 'what a doctorate is' just some sort of semantic exercise? In my view it certainly is not. It has important implications for several areas of practice and policy; for example: the way examiners judge the written dissertation; the wording of university regulations; the viva and the way it is conducted, and which questions should be actually asked; and, last but not least, the question of parity of esteem across the wide range of doctorates now available worldwide.

Thus, the actual interpretation of what a doctorate is, or is deemed to be, is a matter which directly affects student outcomes and students' lives (and, as several studies have shown, the outcome of the assessment process is a very emotional and life changing event: for example, Wellington [2010b]).

It is, and will continue to be, an important question for the many people who take on the following roles:

- As a supervisor (how do I know when a student is 'ready' to submit?)
- As an upgrader/confirmer: is there enough 'mileage' in the upgrade/confirmation review proposal for the student to be allowed to proceed with the doctorate?
- As an internal or an external examiner in deliberating over the various outcomes of the written work and the viva
- And as a member of research degree committees which decide on the wording of regulations, official outcomes of vivas and upgrade/confirmation procedures.

Other categories of person are and also should be asking the question. For example, in this era of accountability, there is a wide range of 'stakeholders' posing the question. Clearly the list of 'stakeholders' includes the student, supervisors, examiners and academics, but increasingly it involves other professionals (for the professional doctorate), and employers for all doctorates. In practice, the answer to the question 'what is a doctorate' depends to a large extent on who is asking, as well as when and where the question is being asked.

Given the variation between doctorates in different parts of the world (Powell and Green 2007; Usher 2002), and the increased (perhaps increasing)

19

number of stakeholders, we are never likely to have complete agreement on the nature of doctorateness. But this is not a good reason for keeping quiet on the issue, or assuming that the notion is best kept tacit or implicit, as I have seen and heard some examiners do (as in 'I know a doctorate when I see one'). This pretence of some sort of unspeakable yet discernible quality is helpful to no one: student, supervisor, examiner, fellow professionals or employers.

SEARCHING FOR THE DOCTORATE: SIX POSSIBLE AREAS

My suggestion is that there are at least six areas of discussion or activity (written or spoken) where we should 'search' for the meaning of the doctorate, and which have a strong bearing on the current assessment of a doctorate and on its future. The six areas that I explore are: the purposes of doctoral study; process versus product; the impact of doctorates; written regulations for the award of the doctorate; the actual face to face examination process; and the voices of those involved in it. These areas are not all of the same category; in particular, the sixth category illustrated in the next chapter is a selection of 'voices' which (I hope) add to the debate in a different way, and in a sense relate to and add to the earlier five. Also, the categories are not mutually exclusive; the overlaps between them are of great importance. In this chapter I take each of the first four areas in turn. In the next chapters I look at the fifth and sixth areas where we might 'search for doctorateness'.

1. *What is the purpose of a doctorate?*

The first way of looking at 'doctorateness' is to take a teleological approach, i.e. to consider what the doctorate is for, what is its purpose?

If one asked a range of research degree students why they had embarked on a doctoral programme, one would be certain to receive a wide range of responses (including, perhaps, a cynical shrug and a comment of 'I really don't know', if you asked that student at the wrong moment). Past research (Scott et al. 2004; Wellington and Sikes 2006) has revealed that students have a vast range of motivations for undertaking a doctorate. Some reasons may be intrinsic and very personal; for example, 'I wanted to prove to myself that I could reach the highest level' (Leonard et al. 2005). Intrinsic motivations can also relate to personal curiosity and interest, or the challenge that doctoral work poses. Equally, motivations can be extrinsic and

20

WHAT IS A DOCTORATE?

related to factors outside of the student's intrinsic desires and goals. For example, some see it as a 'ticket' to either a job or to promotion if they are already employed; some see it as a means to improving their kudos and standing, perhaps in their own work setting or even their home context. Another, closely related, way of reflecting on the teleology of the doctorate is to consider its purposes in terms of outsiders and their interests in it.

Taking intrinsic and extrinsic aspects along with insider and outsider perspectives, the range of purposes for doctoral study could include:

(a) Preparing for a future role or a future career: for example, the doctorate might be seen as producing the next 'batch of researchers', it might be seen as an 'academic apprenticeship' or it might still be seen as a licence to teach (in higher education); equally, and this is especially true in the present context, it might be seen as preparation for industry or other employment.

(b) Those already working might see it as career development or continuing professional development; or it might be seen as a way of researching one's practice, with a view to improving it (especially true of students undertaking a part-time PhD or a professional doctorate).

(c) Some outsiders might regard a doctorate as a vehicle for a person to develop certain generic skills which might then be transferable to other contexts, not least employment. These skills might include problem-solving, researching, writing and communicating; they might be grouped together in a cluster that some like to call 'employability'. This call for the development of generic skills increased since the Roberts Review of 2002 (Roberts 2002); it is a highly debated and contested area, raising such questions as: are these skills genuinely transferable or are they necessarily embedded in a context? Can they be learnt or 'inculcated' out of context? Is the acquisition of these skills a distraction from the main purpose of achieving a doctorate?

(d) The doctorate could be seen largely in terms of a student's personal development and her/his achievement; similarly, it might be viewed in terms of satisfying someone's personal and deeply felt curiosity and intellectual interest in an area or a need to 'prove oneself' (a study by Leonard et al. [2005] showed that this is surprisingly common).

(e) Finally, the purpose of the doctorate might be seen in terms of its product: for example, knowledge production; pushing forward

21

the boundaries of knowledge; adding new or 'original knowledge'; creating a novel position (i.e. a thesis) on an area of research; or generating knowledge which can be 'transferred', to industry, perhaps, or at least disseminated.

2. *Process and product*

These five potential purposes relate to a useful distinction, and often an important tension, when considering the nature of a doctorate. Is it largely about process, i.e. personal development, preparing a person for a career, inculcating certain 'transferable' skills, providing an apprenticeship, giving personal satisfaction and pride? Or is the doctorate mainly concerned with its product, i.e. a body of knowledge, adding to existing work (Park 2007, 32)?

These questions are particularly relevant when it comes to the examination process for the doctorate, i.e. the written dissertation and the oral examination, the viva voce, which we examine later (see Chapter 7). In reading and judging doctoral work there really should be questions about *both* areas: from the process angle, to what extent was the doctoral journey a 'vehicle' for the student's personal development, learning and growth? What skills did the student acquire during the course of the research? Then from the product angle, to what extent is the thesis a contribution to the body of knowledge in an area of study? These distinctions or tensions also appear in written regulations, as we see later.

Incidentally, the tension between process and product also occurs during supervision of doctoral study: the 'complex craft' (Hockey 1997) of supervision should surely be concerned with both. Thus, it is important, during supervision, for everyone involved to reflect on the purposes of 'this particular doctorate' and the motivation behind it. Is it primarily to develop the person, in which case the process is uppermost? Or is it about knowledge production, the 'thesis', and the addition of 'original' knowledge? To what extent are the twin demands of 'process' and 'product' in balance?

In my view, the student and supervisor should attempt to balance the pair and the examiners of the doctorate will be able to determine and ask for themselves whether this has been achieved.

3. *The impact of the doctorate*

A closely related way of looking at the nature of the doctorate is to examine its impact on both the recipient and on other stakeholders who might be

WHAT IS A DOCTORATE?

affected by it. On the face of it, this would seem to be an ideal arena to search for the meaning of doctorateness. Unfortunately, based on my knowledge of the literature, I suggest that this is something which has not been examined in enough depth over the history of the doctorate (interesting exceptions are Leonard et al. [2005] and Maxwell, Evans, and Hickey [2004]). Thus, very few studies have been made of the impact and influence of the doctorate on the student or the wider context to which they 'move' after its completion. This is perhaps surprising given the rise of two recent phenomena: the drive for doctorates to improve the employability and generic/transferable skills of students; and the growth in professional doctorates in various areas such as engineering, health care, business administration and education. The PhD has often been described as an 'apprenticeship' (Park 2005, 2007) but to what extent has this doctoral apprenticeship had an impact on the student and her/his future working life? Similarly, the professional doctorate is founded on a range of statements relating to its impact on professional practice, its role in producing professional knowledge and the goal of developing reflective practitioners or 'researching professionals'.

For example, the Economic and Social Research Council (2005: 93) stated that

> Professional doctorates aim to develop an individual's professional practice and to support them in producing a contribution to (professional) knowledge.

This is a laudable aim but is it realised in practice? Burgess and Wellington (2010) posed the question: to what extent do students who have completed, or are still engaged in, a professional doctorate consider that either the product of their doctorate or the process of doing it, have 'impacted' on their professional practice and development? Their research collected a wide range of case studies or narratives from students who were willing to openly engage in the activity of personal reflection on how the professional doctorate influenced, impacted upon or altered their own professional practice. Data were also collected from written documentation, including evidence from completed professional doctorate theses.

Three main themes emerged in the students' reflections on the impact of their doctorates. First, there is the impact on their professional careers: several narratives revealed an impact in terms of professional career trajectory and impact in the way the students operated as professionals within their work. Some found that completing a professional doctorate significantly changed their work environment, either through rapid promotion to senior posts or in opening up opportunities to undertake research and have their research valued by colleagues.

The second area of impact is on their personal lives: the personal and professional are closely intertwined. The 'personal' influence was felt in at least two areas: the way their own thinking or 'thought processes' developed, and the way they themselves were viewed by their colleagues. For example, several commented on how their writing skills had improved, as did their capacity to think critically and to have greater confidence in their own abilities. This confidence related to a third area of impact: on discourse.

Respondents could state reasons how or why their discourse had changed; this included, for some, the way they responded to others, or listened, as well as a greater understanding of the ways in which language can be a barrier as well as a means of communication. Some reported gaining confidence in their use of language to persuade, change, argue a case, challenge assumptions and listen critically to others.

Overall, in the varying accounts from this study, it is surprising to observe how many students' perceptions of the impact of the doctorate were to do with their own personal development and growth rather than their professional development; certainly, the study indicated few reflections about the development of their profession or 'professional knowledge', as in the Economic and Social Research Council (2005) statement above. The students' perception of being 'more scholarly', 'more aware' and more 'emancipated' links to the concept of the doctorate as professional socialisation (Scott et al. 2004). Is this where doctorateness is to be found? Perhaps, but the type of socialisation found by Burgess and Wellington (2010) did not concern induction into a setting, but rather an enhancement of personal skills, knowledge and confidence to perform at a higher level. This is probably more a result of the process of their doctorate than the product. Interestingly, some of these areas of impact relate to the written regulations that we look at next.

4. *'Doctorateness': what do written regulations say?*

A fourth important way in which we can explore how people perceive and articulate 'doctorateness' is by looking at written regulations (Jackson and Tinkler 2007; Tinkler and Jackson 2004). All universities which offer and examine research degrees in the UK have documents with titles beginning with phrases such as: 'Guidelines for examiners of candidates for ...'; 'Notes for the guidance of research students, supervisors and examiners ...'; 'Notes

WHAT IS A DOCTORATE?

on examination procedures for …'; 'Regulations for degrees of …'; or 'Examination of the thesis; notes for examiners'. Having been an external examiner for research degrees at fifteen of these institutions, I have collected an extensive sample of such documents. It is a valuable exercise to pick out some of the key terms, criteria and descriptors that are written in them. Here is a sample, in no particular order, of some of the key phrases and expressions relating to doctorateness:

- Worthy of publication either in full or abridged form
- Presents a thesis embodying the results of the research
- Original work which forms an addition to knowledge
- Makes a distinct contribution to the knowledge of the subject and offers evidence of originality shown by the discovery of new facts and/or the exercise of independent critical power
- Shows evidence of systematic study and the ability to relate the results of such study to the general body of knowledge in the subject
- The thesis should be a demonstrably coherent body of work
- Shows evidence of adequate industry and application
- Understands the relationship of the special theme of the thesis to a wider field of knowledge
- Represents a significant contribution to learning, for example, through the discovery of new knowledge, the connection of previously unrelated facts, the development of new theory or the revision of older views
- Provides originality and independent critical ability and must contain matter suitable for publication
- Adequate knowledge of the field of study
- Competence in appropriate methods of performance and recording of research
- Ability in style and presentation
- The dissertation is clearly written
- Takes account of previously published work on the subject.

If we examine this list it can be seen that different criteria refer to different aspects of doctorateness. Some refer to the product: 'addition to knowledge', for example. Some refer to process: 'systematic study' or 'adequate industry' can be seen as examples. Some refer to the qualities or abilities or even dispositions of the students themselves: 'critical ability', 'competence in appropriate methods' or 'industry and application'.

25

Others refer to the written thesis and its qualities (part of the product perhaps), with criteria such as 'clearly written' and 'coherent'. Finally, other criteria refer to the next stage, such as suitable or 'worthy' of publication (interestingly, few regulations refer to implication, impact or outcomes other than publication).

From my own experience of trying to put regulations into practice when examining written doctoral dissertations and their oral counterpart, the viva, two important words pose the greatest problems. The first is 'theory', the second 'originality'. Like most problematic words, 'theory' does not lend itself to easy definition and worse, we cannot always recognise one when we see one. The Oxford English Dictionary shows that the word originates from the ancient Greek idea of a *theoria*, a person who acts as a spectator or an envoy, perhaps sent on behalf of a state to consult an oracle. More recently the word theory was taken to mean a mental view or a conception, a system of ideas used, or explanation of a group of facts or phenomena (dated 1638 in the Oxford English Dictionary).

Thus, there is a recurring, continuing debate relating to doctoral work, and especially in the social sciences, over the status, the purpose and the function of theory (Wellington and Szczerbinski 2008, 39). What is its place in the doctorate? Is the presence of theory an essential criterion for doctorateness? These large questions in turn raise more specific ones: where should theory come into doctoral study? Should it be the main 'guiding force', determining the study and its methodology from the outset or should it 'emerge' from the study? Can certain forms of empirical work be conducted without prior theory (in this sense, prior conceptions and theories are said to be 'bracketed' or put to one side)? Or is all research, and all observation, 'theory-laden', as Popper (1968) termed it?

The matter is complicated for students (and supervisors), of course, by lack of agreement over what theory actually is. The issue is complex, but it is an important one for anyone involved in undertaking, supervising and examining research. The discussion of 'theory' is more than a theoretical matter; it is of great practical importance in determining an external examiner's judgement of a dissertation or an oral examination. For example, students are sometimes accused of 'lacking a theoretical framework' or a 'theory base' to their work. Practical outcomes of this accusation could be the requirement to make amendments to or resubmit a thesis, or it could even lead to the non-award of a higher degree. At the next stage, it might even lead to the rejection by a referee of an article submitted for publication. In short, being accused of lacking a theoretical base or, even worse, of being 'a-theoretical', can be practically very serious.

The second word which in my experience creates the most debate before, during and after the examination process is 'originality'. Many universities state that the dissertation should make an 'original contribution'. But what does originality mean?

Phillips and Pugh (2015 for their latest edition) were the first to tackle this question head-on in their discussion of the PhD. They listed numerous ways of being original; their list is actually quite encouraging for anyone who loses sleep at night over whether their work is original or not. This list was adapted in Wellington (2010a, 87–89) as part of a full discussion of different ways of showing originality. To summarise this discussion – the key question is: What forms can an 'original contribution' take? We could list at least seven categories and these are shown in Table 2.1.

The below list of seven categories in which people may be 'original' is intended to be useful in thinking about the assessment of doctoral work. It is also intended to show that the word 'originality', like many words in the regulations sampled above, including 'criticality', is one which is widely used in this context but (again like many) has a range of meanings, few of which are perhaps shared.

TABLE 2.1 Seven ways of being original

- Building new knowledge, e.g. by extending previous work or 'putting a new brick in the wall'
- Using original processes or approaches, e.g. applying new methods or techniques to an existing area of study
- Creating new syntheses, e.g. connecting previous studies or linking existing theories or previous thinkers
- Exploring new implications, for practitioners, policy makers, or theory and theorists
- Revisiting a recurrent issue or debate, e.g. by offering new evidence, new thinking, or a new theory
- Replicating or reproducing earlier work, e.g. from a different place or time, or with a different sample
- Presenting research in a novel way, e.g. new ways of writing, presenting, disseminating.

IN SUMMARY SO FAR …

This chapter has examined the criteria that are used implicitly and explicitly in the assessment of doctorateness. Some of these criteria are stated explicitly, in the form of written regulations and documented criteria for a 'good thesis'. Others, which are often held tacitly, actually emerge or are 'enacted' during the reading of the dissertation and the course of the viva voce. We look closely at these in the following chapters: thus when we examine the types of questioning during the oral examination of a doctoral candidate these tacit or implicit criteria for doctorateness become apparent in a very real way for the student.

My own deliberations in looking at the areas above lead me to think that one, single identifiable, common-to-all quality will never be found or accepted – in much the same way that Wittgenstein gave up the search for inner essences and developed his concept of family resemblances (Wittgenstein 1968, 1981).

However, the absence of an inner essence does not imply that we should not attempt to explore the 'family resemblances'. We owe it to students, supervisors, examiners and employers to remove some of the mystique by trying to make explicit some of the descriptions and characteristics that might appear tacit and implicit. This is what I have attempted to do so far. We need to keep this debate alive, not remain silent about it. The idea of doctorateness is what Gallie (1956) termed an 'essentially contested concept' (he used this label to describe concepts which unavoidably involve 'endless disputes' about their usage which cannot be 'settled by appeal to empirical evidence, linguistic usage, or the canons of logic alone').

This chapter has looked at the key questions which underpin the idea of 'doctorateness', and the regulations and practices which translate this into reality for the doctoral student. I have tried to do this by examining four areas: the purposes of doctorates for different people, the joint issues of process and product, by looking at the possible impact of doctorates and then some of the written regulations used by universities. In the next two chapters I look in more detail at the actual assessment process and the voices of supervisors, examiners and students.

 FURTHER READING

For a study on the alleged 'impact' of doctorates see:

Burgess, H., and J. Wellington. 2010. Exploring the Impact of the Professional Doctorate on Students' Professional Practice and Personal Development: Early Indications. *Work Based Learning E-journal* 1 (1): 160–176.

WHAT IS A DOCTORATE?

For a wide range of discussions on the meaning of 'doctorateness' see:

Denicolo, P., and C. Park. 2010. *Doctorateness an elusive concept?* Gloucester: The Quality Assurance Agency for Higher Education.

Morley, L. 2004. Interrogating Doctoral Assessment. *International Journal of Educational Research* 41 (2): 1–97.

Park, C. 2007. *Redefining the doctorate.* York: Higher Education Academy.

Quality Assurance Agency for Higher Education (QAA). 2004. *Code of practice for the assurance of academic quality and standards in higher education.* Gloucester: QAA.

Sham, M., and H. Green. 2002. Benchmarking the PhD – A Tentative Beginning. *Quality Assurance in Education* 10 (2): 116–124.

WEBSITES

The University of Sheffield has produced an on-line resource for graduate students and staff known as the VGS or Virtual Graduate School, located at:

www.youtube.com/user/vgsschool

One useful video as part of the VGS contains an interview led by Jerry Wellington in which Professor Martin Smith outlines the criteria by which he judges a doctoral thesis and which in turn influence his approach to the viva voce:

www.youtube.com/watch?time_continue=136&v=40AHqiDa5o

(accessed 17/02//2020)

Chapter 3

Enacting 'doctorateness'
Doctoral examining in practice

THE EXAMINATION PROCESS: HOW IS THE JUDGEMENT OF 'DOCTORATENESS' PLAYED OUT IN PRACTICE?

Clearly, the two embodiments or enactments of a doctorate are the written dissertation and then the viva voce or oral examination; these are the two ways in which the doctorate becomes real, tangible and audible.

There are clearly dangers in using the examination process as a means of providing insight into the nature of doctorateness, certainly if we are looking for an essential meaning for the term. A range of literature has pointed out the variability in examination processes across universities (Jackson and Tinkler 2001; Tinkler and Jackson 2002); others have examined the variability in vivas both within (Hartley and Fox 2002; Morley, Leonard, and David 2002) and across disciplines (Trafford 2003). Denicolo (2003) has helpfully examined no less than thirteen aspects of the examination process in which there is variation, ranging from the expertise of the examiners to the relative weight put on the viva and the very purpose of the oral examination.

Park (2005, 196) sums it up neatly by saying that 'the doctoral examination can be viewed as a socially constructed encounter rather than a fully objective and impartial process'. This neat summary also sums up the concept of doctorateness; that too is a socially constructed concept, and therefore subject to interpretations, hence my suggestion in this book that we look at it from a variety of angles or perspectives.

Can we begin to unpack or unpick what a 'doctorate' is by considering these two realisations of it? My answer is yes.

30

WRITTEN CRITERIA FOR DOCTORAL AWARDS

Beginning with the dissertation, one university handbook gives a full page on the criteria relating to both the thesis itself and the individual chapters and what they might contain. Thus, the handbook suggests that there might be individual chapters on the context of the study, the literature, the methodology and methods, the design of the study, the analysis of the findings, the results or outcomes of the study, a discussion of these outcomes and their limitations, and finally a chapter on the conclusions. As for the thesis 'as a whole', the handbook puts forward criteria in six areas, some of which relate to process and others to product. They require that the thesis should be:

- Authentic: it should be the student's own work, and all sources should be fully acknowledged and referenced
- Scholarly: it should meet the usual norms of 'scholarship' (what some have called the academic virtues);
- Showing 'critical discrimination' and a 'sense of proportion' in 'evaluating the evidence and opinions of others'
- Professional: the thesis should show evidence of a repertoire of research skills;
- Appropriate to a professional researcher and a good understanding of the 'role of such a researcher'
- Well structured, written and presented, in an 'orderly and coherent way'.

THE VIVA VOCE AS AN ENACTMENT OF DOCTORATENESS?

What about the oral examination, when the search for doctorateness reaches its end point: how do examiners approach it and what kinds of questions tend to be asked?

There is an increasing body of literature on the viva, its purpose and its conduct. This is to be welcomed after a time in which the viva was seen as something mysterious, and very much an event behind closed doors which needed to be 'unveiled' (Burnham 1994; Hartley and Jory 2000). It still is a closed event in the UK and other countries but, from my reading of the literature on vivas (Trafford [2003] and Wallace [2002] are particularly

31

revealing) and my own experiences of around sixty of them, I feel that a number of areas of questioning are and should be followed in trying to decide whether a study is at doctoral level (reassuringly, most of them relate to the regulations sampled above).

For example, the 'thesis', meaning position, is almost certain to be discussed. The type of question here might be: 'please could you summarise your thesis?' What are the main findings of your research? What would somebody from this field learn from reading your thesis that they didn't know before? What did you learn from doing it?

Other areas which usually are, and certainly should, be explored in assessing 'doctorateness' are:

(1) Theory: as discussed earlier, a doctoral thesis is concerned with ideas and theories so it would be a strange viva that did not raise this discussion. Questions might take this form: 'What theories/theoretical frameworks/perspectives have you drawn upon in your research? Which were most valuable? Why these and not others? Which theories did your study illuminate, if any?'

(2) The literature review: this should also form an area for discussion in a good viva, and questions might include: 'What shaped or guided your literature review? Why did it cover the areas that it did? (And not others.) Why did/didn't you include the work of X in your study? Did you conduct a systematic review of the literature? If so, which criteria for inclusion did you use?'

(3) Methodology and research approach: typical questions on these areas might be:

'Why did you employ the methods you used? Why not others, e.g. X? What informed your choice of methods? What would you do differently, with hindsight?'

(4) Ethics: if students have carried out fieldwork as part of their study then they really should be asked about ethical issues, for example: 'Which ethical issues did you encounter before, during and after your research? How did you ensure the confidentiality and anonymity of your respondents? How did you inform them about your research and gain their consent?'

(5) Again, if fieldwork of any kind was conducted (interviews, focus groups, surveys, observation), the business of sampling should be raised in the viva: 'Why did you select the sample you did? Can you

see any problems with it? If it is a small-scale study, can you justify why so few were involved?'

(6) Data analysis is another area that should be discussed and questions might follow these lines: 'Did anything surprise you in the data ("hit you in the face")? Any anomalies? How did you analyse your data? How did you categorise/filter the data? Did themes emerge from your data (a posteriori) or did you bring them to the data (a priori)? Why did you analyse it in this way? Could the analysis have been done in another way?'

(7) Generalisability: viva questions might be of the form: 'How far do think you can generalise from your work? What lessons can be learnt from it by practitioners/policy makers/other researchers?' Similarly, students might well be asked: 'What are the key messages and implications of your research study?'

(8) Finally, at some stage in a good viva students should be asked to reflect on the strengths and limitations of their study. This may then lead to two final sets of questions: one about which aspects of the work could be taken further and how, and another about possible publication, e.g. students might be asked: 'Which elements of your work do you feel are worthy of publication and/or presentation at a conference? What plans do you have for publication and dissemination?'

VOICES ON 'DOCTORATENESS': WHAT DO PEOPLE SAY?

We have seen some of the written regulations which attempt to 'make explicit' what a doctorate should be. We have considered the lines of questioning which are followed in the practice of conducting the viva. This section is rather different: what do individuals actually say when asked about the nature of the doctorate? I carried out a series of one-to-one interviews with an opportunistic sample of six experienced supervisors and examiners, and asked them to express their personal views and perspectives on 'doctorateness'. I also carried out face-to-face interviews with six doctoral students, again an opportunistic sample, each lasting about half an hour. I am not claiming that any of the views reported below are representative; I am simply claiming that these were the perspectives expressed to me.

The supervisor's and examiner's perspectives

I can only report a small number of viewpoints here. These are all taken from Wellington, 2013. One experienced supervisor was at first reluctant to go beyond intuition:

> You know it when you see it – often I've seen Master's work that I've thought is doctoral level. It's intuitive and tacit.

But this supervisor and examiner then went on to say:

> They've got to show evidence of critical reflection.
> .... It's about not taking things for granted and questioning assumptions.
> Good writing is increasingly important for me as a criterion for 'doctorateness'; you should be communicating your knowledge clearly.

Another supervisor, also an experienced examiner, felt that a doctoral student is an 'apprentice', but that this notion may be different in the professional doctorate:

> It's an apprenticeship in doing research, in the social sciences anyway. Somebody is going on a journey, even in a professional doctorate although this is a more restricted form, it's more tightly bounded. They are a different sort of apprentice, they need even more supervision. Some find it difficult to really engage with the fact that this is a piece of research, they start by seeing it more as a professional report and that makes it quite difficult to shape it.

Finally, another supervisor, when asked what a doctorate is, told me:

> I could trot out the usual responses but I actually think it's more than that in my area, it's a huge journey, a journey that you've no idea what you face when you start. It's a hugely challenging personal journey which brings into relief sometimes many issues that you thought you could leave behind but can't.

The student's perspective

I would guess that there are as many student views on what a doctorate is as there are students. I quote only two of my student interviewees here, as illustrations. Interestingly, for both, the doctorate is a very personal matter which ties in with much of the previous literature on students' motivations and perceptions (e.g. Leonard et al. 2005; Wellington and Sikes 2006):

It means that you're really clever.

… for me, it's a way of proving to myself that I must be clever, because I never feel it. Somehow this certificate will prove it. But the other thing is that I love my subject.

I want to show that I've got a deep knowledge of my subject and I could be called an 'expert' on it.

Its intrinsic worth is the main thing for me. It's such a gift to be able to spend three years or more doing something that you absolutely love, and it's your job to be passionately interested in it. I'm enjoying doing it because it's such an opportunity. It means so much to me because it's such a privilege to be able to do it.

When I asked the same students for their views on the criteria for 'doctorateness' they said:

It shows that you can argue a case and that your argument is supported by rigorous research and evidence, without any flaws (or huge flaws anyway). It's rather like law, when you present the case for and against something.

If other people read it, it changes their thinking, it gets them to think differently, to see things in a different way even if it's just for that moment when they're reading it to expand people's perceptions and the way they see things.

We discussed the notion of originality earlier, but as it is such a key notion in considering 'doctorateness', I leave the final word on this topic with one supervisor and one student, who both expressed in their own way the view that the notion of originality is a problematic one. First, from the supervisor's and examiner's perspective:

Originality? I think a lot of students are put off by that word. They think 'well, I'm not going to discover penicillin' or 'I'm not going to be able to do these things'. But once they realise that it's their study, then the originality itself will be in there and they've got to draw it out. If the student and the supervisors have done their jobs together, that originality should be there anyway, it should emerge from the study. It needn't be about a substantive issue, it may be about methodology, or often both.

And, second, from a student's perspective:

I think it's actually different for medical research when you make a breakthrough and the treatment of x, y or z will never be the same again because of this particular breakthrough, but when you're dealing with ideas ... it is kind of unlikely that one person will have a totally new idea. There's something in the ether about ways of thinking that everyone picks up on and we all start to think in those ways anyway. Subtle influences all around us live in a cultural milieu, with centuries of thinking. You can't separate yourself out from that. Who knows where all your 'influences' come from? It depends on the context you are in (in time and space).

IN CONCLUSION: WHAT SORT OF A QUESTION IS 'WHAT IS A DOCTORATE'? WHY IS IT DIFFICULT TO GET A STRAIGHT ANSWER TO THIS QUESTION?

In this and the previous chapter I have looked at several areas in which examiners might find evidence of 'doctorateness'. Each area reveals a different aspect – rather like the proverb of the group examining an elephant where one feels its trunk, another ears and another legs – each person is sensing a different facet of the beast.

Before moving to the next chapter, it is now time to consider what kind of a question is being asked here. What questions is it like? Is it like asking: what does it mean to be 'British' or what does it mean 'to be human'? Is it more like the question: what is an animal or what is a plant? So, for example, by asking it are we searching for some sort of inner, essential quality that characterises 'doctorateness' (like 'human-ness' or 'Britishness')? My own view is that to search for a single, common meaning belonging to all doctorates is rather like looking for the Holy Grail: our chances of success are quite slim. We should give up a search for some sort of 'inner essence' of doctorateness. In Wittgenstein's later work (1981) he gave up the search for essential meanings and denotations, and suggested two key concepts: first, the idea of family resemblances, discussed shortly; and second, the idea that the meaning of a word or a term is found in its use.

36

The latter idea suggests that instead of looking for the essential meaning of doctorateness we should look at various aspects, facets, behaviours, opinions, usages, enactments and activities that surround the doctoral endeavour, and use these to examine the evolving nature of doctoral study. This is what I have tried to do in the areas discussed in these chapters although there may well be more. In this way we can attempt to discern certain 'family resemblances' which link doctorates together rather than some inner, core meaning or essence which is common to all. Wittgenstein discusses the nature of concepts and what makes them (in my words) 'hang together'. He uses the example of games and the concept of a game. Consider a wide spectrum of examples of games: dominoes, chess, hopscotch, football, cricket, tiddlywinks, PlayStation games and Trivial Pursuit (these are my examples, not his). Do they all have certain characteristics in common? Well, some might: e.g. cricket and football both have eleven players in a team and they use a ball. But others do not. Games have what Wittgenstein called a 'family resemblance'.

As a result of these resemblances, we can recognise a game when we see one (so if we went to a new country and saw two people pushing plastic tokens around on a board we might ask: 'what's their game?'). But we would find it hard to define 'game'.

My view is that doctorateness is rather like this. Park (2007, 5), in discussing the variability in doctoral degrees now prevalent, suggests that 'logically, there should be something identifiable and widely accepted as doctorateness in all the forms'. But the linking factors are, in my view, not some kind of inner essence but family resemblances across the wide spectrum of doctorates that now exist.

I would like to finish this chapter on a personal and perhaps pragmatic note. From my own experience of examining doctorates, the single most necessary (though not on its own sufficient) quality that makes up a doctorate is the notion of a 'contribution', without the complication of the adjectives 'original' or publishable. The key criteria would then be: provided that the doctoral dissertation (and its live version, the viva voce) have a thesis in the sense of a position and an argument, has the thesis made a contribution to the field of study? Has it built on previous arguments and theses (from previous literature) and pushed it forward a little or added to it? Does it provide another 'brick in the wall'? Will this contribution potentially make an impact or bring about a change in thinking and to theory, policy, or practice?

37

FURTHER READING

For other discussions of PhD 'quality', criteria for judgement and the assessment of 'doctorateness', see:

Bourke, S. 2007. PhD Thesis Quality. *South African Journal of Higher Education* 21 (8): 1042–1052.

Denicolo, P. 2003. Assessing the PhD. *Quality Assurance in Education* 11 (2): 84–91.

Lovat, T. 2004. Ways of Knowing in Doctoral Examination: How Examiners Position Themselves in Relation to the Doctoral Candidate. *Australian Journal of Educational and Developmental Psychology* 4: 126–145.

Mullins, G., and M. Kiley. 2002. "It's a PhD, Not a Nobel Prize': How Experienced Examiners Assess Research Theses. *Studies in Higher Education* 27 (4): 369–386.

Tinkler, P., and C. Jackson. 2000. Examining the Doctorate. *Studies in Higher Education* 25: 167–180.

WEBSITES

QAA. 2015. *Characteristics statement: Doctoral degree*. Gloucester: QAA

www.qaa.ac.uk/docs/qaa/quality-code/doctoral-degree-characteristics-15.pdf?sfvrsn=50aef981_10 (accessed 17/02/2020)

Thesis whisperer: this is a well-established website, set up in Australia, of interest to students, supervisors and examiners. It has many insightful and provocative comments from around the world:

https://thesiswhisperer.com/ (accessed 27/04/2020)

Vitae also have some interesting comments and anecdotes on doctoral examining and the viva, for example:

www.vitae.ac.uk/doing-research/doing-a-doctorate/completing-your-doctorate/your-viva

Part II

Practical aspects of the doctoral examining process

Chapter 4

Who are the examiners and what do they look for?

THE USUAL CHRONOLOGY IN THE EXAMINATION OF DOCTORAL WORK

Figure 4.1 below shows the pathway that the doctoral examining process is likely to take. This figure should not be taken too literally as there may be some variations in the chronological order, just as there are variations along the way between regulations, practices and criteria across universities.

The figure shows that in some cases and countries there is no viva voce and hence the deviation shown to the usual pathway in the UK. This is also the reason why Chapter 7 of this book is placed late in the book and is in some ways a 'stand-alone' chapter.

The figure also shows that the choice of who the examiners should be is made at an early stage, usually before final submission, and is thus of primary importance in the chronology.

CHOOSING EXAMINERS: HOW ARE THEY CHOSEN ... INCLUDING WHY YOU?

The first decision to be made in the doctoral examination process is: who will be the examiners for it? In many ways this level of choice or autonomy in higher education assessment is unique, i.e. very different from under-graduate or Master's level examination. Thus the choice of examiners is a vital choice: its importance for student, supervisor and then the examiners cannot be overstated.

The ways and means by which examiners are chosen for a doctorate are many and varied. For example, the choice may be made based on whom the supervisor is familiar with and who has been seen to be thorough and profes-sional in the past. Second, the examiner may be chosen as someone who is

41

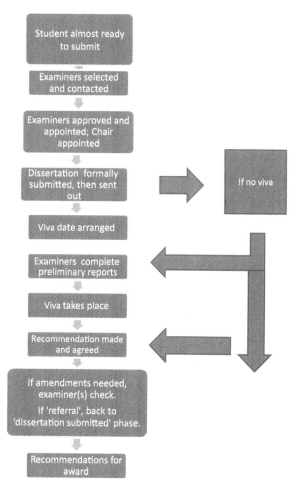

FIGURE 4.1 The likely examination process

clearly an expert in the field of the student's doctorate. This may be on the basis of the methodological field or the field of study (a point we return to later). This is not always a good idea incidentally – the expert in the field may not always be the ideal examiner.

On a more cynical level, the way in which examiners are chosen may be less than professional, explicit or above board. The supervisor may know someone who owes the department (or the supervisor) a favour from an

THE EXAMINERS AND WHAT THEY LOOK FOR

event in the past. This might apply both internally and externally. The department may know someone externally who has acted for that department as an external previously and is seen as (to use metaphors that I have heard) a 'safe pair of hands', a 'soft touch' or at least 'not an ogre'. It helps if one knows that the visiting external is not pompous, unlikely to 'behave badly' or come to the department with all sorts of 'bees in her/his bonnet' (again a metaphor that I have heard used in staffroom conversations).

Who should make the choice? Sometimes the supervisor will choose them without consulting the student. However, my own preference as a supervisor (and examiner) has always been to involve the student in the decision on whom to approach as both internal and external examiner(s) – although the final decision and of course the invitation must come from a member of staff. The criteria I would suggest as the best factors by which to make the choice would be:

- Will the examiners be sympathetic towards the student's research and methodology?
- Will they be familiar with this field? (even if they are not a perceived national expert in it – see above)
- If the doctorate is a Prof Doc has at least one of them examined a doctorate of this nature before? Does the examiner have some affinity, familiarity and support for the professional doctorate?
- Are the examiners (internal and external) likely to be fair, civilised, thorough and challenging without being aggressive or overbearing?
- Will they come to the thesis and the viva (if there is one) with their own agendas?
- Finally, how well will the combination of the two or three examiners work? How is the 'chemistry' between them? Will they function well together in pre-planning, in planning and conducting the viva, asking questions and finally deciding on an agreed final report and recommendations? Complementarity is needed, not conflict.

I put forward these criteria from a supervisor's and student's point of view but they are highly relevant for examiners to consider, either before they accept the invitation to examine or after that decision in planning for the examination. The choice of examiners is a vitally important one for student and supervisor – it needs and will require considerable thought and time for reflection. I have examined many a doctorate when this has clearly not happened and it soon becomes apparent, either at the thesis reading stage or at the viva voce. The complexity, implicit thinking and complication that

43

PRACTICAL ASPECTS OF THE EXAMINING PROCESS

TABLE 4.1 Good and bad qualities in examiners at doctoral level

QUALITIES TO SEEK	CHARACTERISTICS TO AVOID
Fair, civil	Pompous, aggressive, uncivil, arrogant
Competent, thorough	'sketchy', superficial
No hidden agendas	Lots of bees in the bonnet; dogmatic
Can establish future connections and networks; 'unlocking doors'	Disrespectful of the student
Confident in their own judgement	Dogmatic, full of themselves
Supportive	Overzealous, over critical, dismissive
Asks clear questions (in the viva) and listens carefully; not over hasty	Does not ask questions, engages in long monologues during the viva; rushes the oral

occur in choosing examiners are factors that will have a huge bearing on the doctoral assessment process.

Thus the choice, and how it has been made, is as important for the invited external and internal examiners as it is for student and supervisor. 'Why me?' is a question that every examiner should ask when the invitation arrives! As a summary, I suggest that the good and bad qualities of a doctoral examiner are shown in brief in Table 4.1.

I have presented Table 4.1 in the context of how and why examiners are (or should be) chosen. We return to these same characteristics when we discuss in detail how the written thesis is analysed and judged and how (where this applies) a viva voce is conducted.

Incidentally, with the growth of the professional doctorate and the 'economic imperative' in all doctorates, the idea of having at least one examiner from employment, industry, or the professions was widely touted. In practice, this has rarely happened.

CHECKING NATIONAL AND LOCAL FRAMEWORKS

We have already looked at written regulations for doctorates and examined them in the context of a 'search for doctorateness'. But it is worth emphasising that every country has its own set of criteria and standards for the award

THE EXAMINERS AND WHAT THEY LOOK FOR

of a doctorate so it is essential that examiners (plus supervisor and student) should check which national statements on 'doctoral degree characteristics' apply to their own context. For example, in Britain the QAA has its own 'quality code' at the following address:

www.qaa.ac.uk/docs/qaa/quality-code/doctoral-degree-characteristics-15.pdf?sfvrsn=50aef981_10

Other countries will have theirs; for example, in Denmark the following guidelines can be found on assessment:

https://healthsciences.ku.dk/research/doctoral-degree-ku/guidelines/Guideline_for_the_assessment_of_a_doctoral_thesis_04122018.pdf

At more local levels each university will have its own documents on doctoral examining, for example: Massey University

www.massey.ac.nz/massey/fms/Research/Guidelines%20for%20Examiners%20of%20Doctoral%20Thesis%20Involving%20Creative%20Works.pdf?831958F480ABD763D8FCDF3FBACB3075

Aarhus University includes in its regulations the need for a public 'defense', as they and the Americans often call the oral examination. This is something we discuss in Chapter 7.

http://phd.au.dk/fileadmin/grads.au.dk/HE/Forms_and_templates/Rules_and_regulations/Rules_and_regulations_2016/03102016_Guidelines_for_assessment_-_PhD_dissertation_and_public_defense.pdf

The University of Leicester provide guidance and documentation which is very impressive:

www2.le.ac.uk/offices/lli/developing-learning-and-teaching/enhance/quality/external-examiners

Enough examples: needless to say it is vital that you check your own HEI rules, guidance and regulations for the criteria for 'doctorateness' and for the procedures that must be followed, as they do vary from one HEI to another, e.g. in whether or not an independent Chair is required, and whether there is one internal and one external or perhaps two externals. Always check. Equally, if one is invited to be an external at another HEI then it goes without saying that you should check all their documents on criteria and assessment procedures.

READING THE THESIS ONCE IT ARRIVES ON YOUR DESK – WHERE DO PEOPLE START?

Currently, examiners receive a hard copy of the final submission as well as, often, an electronic version. This is considered to be good practice as it is neither good for the examiner's eyesight nor conducive to careful, detailed

45

PRACTICAL ASPECTS OF THE EXAMINING PROCESS

examination to have only screen/soft copy. Equally, soft copy is valuable for other reasons such as checking word lengths and websites or easily checking on References listed in 'clickable' format. The electronic copy can also be valuable if (say) animation or video is being submitted; or if colour versions of diagrams/tables/figures are used to enhance presentation or interpretation and the hard copy is in black and white.

I always wonder which pages examiners turn to first when the print on paper dissertation of around seventy or eighty thousand words or more, weighing about three kilos, arrives with a thump on their desk. So I always ask them.

The most common response and mine too is (not surprisingly) the Abstract. This is a real indicator of what is to come. On a pedantic note, if it contains typing errors then alarm bells start to ring. Seen from the student's and the supervisor's angle, it is vitally important that the Abstract is free of typos. This may mean checking it over, and reading it out loud, four or five times but it is well worth the time and effort. Believe me, if there are typing errors and poorly constructed or ungrammatical sentences in the few hundred words of an Abstract then the examiner will be on alert for the entirety of the thesis. In some ways that is a pity as it may distract from the content, but a good examiner should be able to evaluate the content and arguments in a doctorate even whilst distracted by the technical side of the writing. Spell checkers are fine but they are not the sole answer. Yet, many students are almost dependent upon them.

Moving on from Pedant's corner, the Abstract should indicate clearly the content that is to come. It is a summary of the thesis and therefore should match up with the arguments and the conclusions which will follow (believe it or not, such consistency is not always the case). Technically, it should not really contain references or quotations though I have seen this happen. As an examiner I will look for:

- Why was this study made?
- Why is it important? What is its significance?
- What was actually done?
- How was it done and why this way?
- What are the key findings and how do they form a 'contribution'?

It is extremely difficult to write a good, clear Abstract using a maximum of (in some cases) only 400 words. It is something that needs to be drafted, checked, read aloud, re-drafted and drafted again over several cycles or

46

THE EXAMINERS AND WHAT THEY LOOK FOR

iterations. An examiner can tell fairly quickly if this has been done – and in many cases it will be the first page that they read.

What do other examiners look for either first or at an early stage? Some look at the contents list but a surprising number turn straight to the back of the hefty document to see the list of References. When I told one of my doctoral students that this is the second chunk of text that I turn to, she said: is that to see if your name has been included? Well actually it's not, even though some examiners may enjoy seeing themselves cited (myself included I hesitate to add). The serious reason for going quickly to the References is to see what the doctoral student's own work has been based on. What literature has the study used as a foundation or a launching pad (if those are the correct metaphors)? Are there any unusual references and items of reading, things that I may not have seen before, that I can learn from? Or are there just the 'usual suspects'? How much previously published work has been delved into? What is the length of the list? It may look rather short so the examiner will need to explore the reasons for this. If the Reference list is excessively long the examiner may become suspicious and will be tempted to check if all publications cited have has been utilised and to what extent.

Different examiners will have different favourites as starting points. The examples used above are just some personal favourites and some of the 'diving in points' that others have told me about. There is no right or wrong place to start reading a dissertation. It is a long job as argued in the next section.

MANAGING YOUR TIME AS AN EXAMINER

The first question, that I don't have a clear answer to, is: how long could you and should you take in reading the submission? It varies.

I am acting as external examiner for two doctoral dissertations at the moment. My brain is only capable of reading one at a time and I will wait until the first one has been examined before I start to read the second. The one I am working on currently has turned out to be well written, clearly structured and with a strong argument running through it. The literature review seems thorough and critical and the Reference list is much as I would expect it to be, with the occasional interesting surprise (i.e. not just all the usual suspects). When I next have a spare hour I will write the preliminary report and send it off to the HEI. How long will all this have taken? Well, I like to read every word and every sentence – if a sentence does not make sense to me then I will mention it in my report. (Equally, if a sentence is

47

PRACTICAL ASPECTS OF THE EXAMINING PROCESS

long, convoluted and full of lots of big words I will make a note of it, so that the student can clarify it for me.)

The work I am currently examining is a 'good read' and very engaging, which does help. It has very few typos. I estimate that in total I will have spent around twenty to twenty-five hours on it prior to the viva. Incidentally, the fee I am paid as external for this is £175. Add another 8 hours for travel time to the viva, conducting the oral and then agreeing a final report with the internal – after tax on the fee that works out at just under £5 per hour. This is well below the current minimum wage so I am definitely not doing it for the money (see Chapter 1 for examiners' reasons for saying Yes). Incidentally, in most universities, the internal examiner does not get paid (over and above her usual salary) but there is a small minority where a token fee is paid to internals. I have mixed feelings on this but won't go into it here.

WHAT MAKES A 'GOOD' DOCTORAL THESIS?

Whenever I examine a doctorate I always ask the other examiner(s), sad character that I am, what qualities they see as making up a good thesis.

What do they say? The most common response given to me (so I claim no generalisability here) is that it shows evidence of 'criticality'. It contains critical thinking and critical analysis. People rarely go on to explain what 'being critical' means exactly, almost as if its meaning is taken for granted and goes without saying (rather like the discussion of 'doctorateness' in earlier chapters when people say that they know it when they see it). I explore the meaning of criticality later. But first, what are the other qualities that people tell me they look for. I have not done a quantitative analysis of their responses (perhaps I should have done) but they are roughly in this order, using a mixture of adjectives and nouns:

- Clear and concise/clarity of thought
- Focused, with clear aims and objectives
- Ethical
- Coherent and cohesive (slightly elusive terms, perhaps)
- Reader friendly, readable, fluent
- Relevant to the contemporary situation
- Has the aim of improving the current situation
- Answers its research questions! (often said with an implied exclamation mark)

THE EXAMINERS AND WHAT THEY LOOK FOR

- Has a clear and logical structure ('it is not a detective story'); well organised, easy to navigate
- Well written, well presented, good sentence structure
- The conclusions connect with the evidence (they don't 'over stretch')
- 'It does what it says on the tin'
- Not overambitious
- Makes a contribution, adds to the body of knowledge.

IN SUMMARY ...

These qualities and criteria have all been said to me – there are many more. I could go on but I won't at this point. I summarise this section and the chapter by showing a table, partly based on the above points, which I use as a checklist when reading a doctoral dissertation (see Table 4.2).

Finally, and perhaps most importantly, the examiner should always look closely at the research questions which guide the dissertation. How many are there? Are they all answerable? Are they answerable in the student's lifetime?

TABLE 4.2 Qualities to look for in a 'good' thesis

The 'best' theses
- Consider a wide range of literature (including at least one or two references which make the reader say 'Ah! That's a new one')
- Are well-structured and clear to follow
- Ensure that every sentence makes sense
- Do not contain non sequiturs, i.e. sentences which make the reader wonder: 'where did that come from?'
- Embed their own work in the work of others
- Deliberate on methods and methodology before their own empirical work
- Are honest and open about the methods they have used, and why
- Reflect back on their methods and methodology after they have reported their work
- Contain few typos, clumsy sentences or incorrect use of words (e.g., 'effect' for 'affect', 'it's' for 'its', 'criterion' for 'criteria')
- Make fully explicit the lessons which can be learnt from their research
- Bring out their own limitations (without being apologetic) and suggest areas for further research
- Pull out practical implications for policy-makers or practitioners or both
- Contribute to the 'public store of knowledge'- even, perhaps, the 'public good' not just the writer's own personal development.

49

Examiners will sometimes see questions of the ilk: why does a pig have four legs? This is perhaps not a good example but this type of question will always make the examiners think — can this ever be answered? To most examiners, the best doctoral dissertations have clear research questions — not too numerous and not too ambitious — and the main focus of the doctoral study is to *address* these questions to the best of the students' ability, within the limits of their resources and time, even if they are not definitively answered.

 FURTHER READING

Articles from a range of perspectives in the UK and worldwide provide a spectrum of views on the work of examiners, the recommendations they make and the activity of 'being an examiner':

Bourke, S. 2007. PhD Thesis Quality. *South African Journal of Higher Education* 21 (8): 1042–1052.

Bourke, S., and A. Holbrook. 2013. Examining PhD and Research Masters Theses. *Assessment & Evaluation in Higher Education* 38 (4): 407–416on.

Carter, S. 2008. Examining the Doctoral Thesis. *Innovations in Education and Teaching International* 45 (4): 365–374.

Denicolo, P. 2003. Assessing the PhD. *Quality Assurance in Education* 11 (2): 84–91.

Grabbe, L. 2003. The Trials of Being a PhD External Examiner. *Quality Assurance in Education* 11 (2): 128–133.

Mullins, G., and M. Kiley. 2002. "It's a PhD, Not a Nobel Prize': How Experienced Examiners Assess Research Theses. *Studies in Higher Education* 27 (4): 369–386.

Pearce, L 2005. *How to examine a thesis*. Maidenhead: Open University Press.

Tinkler, P., and C. Jackson. 2000. Examining the Doctorate. *Studies in Higher Education* 25: 167–180.

Chapter 5

Preparing the preliminary, independent reports

WHAT IS THE PURPOSE OF THE INDEPENDENT REPORT AND HOW IS IT SHAPED BY THE WRITTEN THESIS?

The preliminary report is a document that must be completed independently by each examiner prior to moving towards a final, agreed report. It is vital that examiners should do this without conferring, hence the name for many universities of the 'independent report'. The examiners' reports cannot be seen by either student or supervisor in advance of the viva or the completion of the final reports. The main purpose of the preliminary report is to signal any perceived 'concerns' or issues, to foresee any problems that might occur and to prepare for the forthcoming viva.

What should it contain? Well, the university for whom I am examining at the moment provides a template (see Table 5.1) which poses several questions and then allows the examiner to expand and comment further. Since the work being examined will also be judged orally, then it is highly advisable (and sometimes requested) for each examiner to suggest the issues they would like to explore in the viva, areas they would like to have clarified and even specific questions they wish to pose during the event.

What makes a good independent report?

With some universities the preliminary report will not be structured by headings or questions – they will simply ask for an assessment of the written work submitted. For example, the examiner may be given space on an electronic form with guidance such as:

> Please provide your independent assessment of the candidate's thesis including a consideration of whether the candidate has demonstrated a

51

broad knowledge and understanding of their discipline and its associated research techniques, the application of these, strengths and weaknesses in the thesis and any particular issues that you wish to draw out in the oral examination.

In another university (University of Leicester) examiners are told that they are 'required to complete an independent assessment of the thesis before the viva exam takes place'. This should:

- Consider whether the research student has demonstrated a broad knowledge and understanding of their discipline and its associated research techniques
- Assess whether the research student has applied the techniques, as appropriate, to their thesis
- Summarise the main argument of the thesis
- Comment on its strengths and weaknesses
- Highlight any particular issues that the examiners would like to draw out in the viva exam.

This university also gives guidance for examiners of a practice-based doctorate:

Where the practical element of a practice-based degree is being considered, the pre-viva report should consider both the thesis and the practical element. If examiners have 'Particular concerns/queries' that they would like to raise before the viva exam takes place they should be raised via the Graduate School Office.

In many pre-viva reports, the template will pose a series of questions (as in Table 5.1) and also allow room for the open ended comments and space to suggest the areas that need to be covered in the viva.

I have known many examiners who have gone to enormous trouble to list all the typographical errors that the student has 'committed'. As a result, the preliminary report has run into four or five pages. To me this seems a huge burden on the examiner and a waste of valuable time. If there are errors in the writing they must be corrected but it is not the examiners' job to point out every one (it is certainly not something to engage in during a good viva either). The onus for this level of correction must surely belong to the student, perhaps with help from the supervisor.

Personally, I think a good preliminary report should be clear and succinct, it should lead up to the viva (if there is to be one) and it should be formative as well as summative. Two sides of A4 should be ample for this.

52

PREPARING PRELIMINARY, INDEPENDENT REPORTS

TABLE 5.1 Examples of questions that might occur in the prelim report

Does the dissertation represent a significant contribution to knowledge of the subject by?

(a) the discovery of new facts?
and/or
(b) the exercise of independent critical powers?

Does the written work show evidence of originality?

Is the written submission satisfactory in respect of literary presentation, clarity and succinctness?
Is the abstract acceptable?
Which areas do you wish to explore during the oral examination?

Table 5.1 is intended as a kind of collage of the type of questions that tend to be in most preliminary reports. You can see from this table that several issues tend to appear in every case: the issue of whether the work does contribute to knowledge in its field; the question of criticality and the 'exercise of critical powers'; the related issue of independence or independent 'thought' in some cases; the age-old question, explored earlier, about the O word – originality; and, the question of how well the dissertation (or portfolio or collection of published work) is written and presented. The latter, in most cases, includes the question of technical issues such as punctuation and typos. Finally, an indication of how the viva might proceed is useful at this stage as it helpfully sets the scene for the pre-viva, face-to-face meeting that occurs between examiners and the Chair (if there is one).

Incidentally, some universities will ask the examiners to state clearly (and with reasons) in their preliminary report whether or not the university should proceed with the viva voce. I will not name names but this has happened to me twice as an external (I said Yes in both cases!).

PROCESS AND PRODUCT IN THE EXAMINER'S REPORT

I have already argued in Chapter 2 that the essence of 'doctorateness' should include process as well as product. In some ways the written dissertation is the product of the doctorate in its entirety. It is the culmination of a lot of hard work, brain energy, emotional ups and downs, and several years of learning and

53

personal growth. Yet all the examiner sees, reads and holds is the written output, the heavy tome on top of your desk. Behind this is the process of achieving a doctorate and producing this written document. In some ways this is hidden or tacit and indeed often neglected. In my view, it is our duty as examiners to consider the process the student has undergone as well as the product visible before us. Hence, I feel that to some extent this should figure in the preliminary report. In a good dissertation, some discussion of 'process' should be part of the written submission – probably as a reflection in the last chapter. In addition, exploring and discussing process and personal development should be part of the viva – hence the expression of support for the viva that I offer in Chapter 7, not least as a way of allowing the student to shine and tell her story.

A KEY ELEMENT IN THE REPORT: THE IMPORTANCE OF BEING CRITICAL

This is a vitally important element of 'doctorateness' and the examining process, so I have devoted a large paragraph below to examine what exactly examiners might be looking for here.

In my experience as an examiner and a supervisor, the most commonly used word is 'critical'. During supervision, students are regularly urged to be 'more critical'. This urging usually refers to their literature review, to their reflection on methods and methodology, to their analysis and interpretation of findings/data, or to their reflection on the whole study in the last chapter of the dissertation. As examiners, we also look for criticality in precisely those areas. Hence the need to 'be critical' is not only a key element in supervision but most importantly for this book it is a quality and a key criterion when examiners judge doctoral work. So the term is commonly used but not always made explicit to students. So what is it that we are looking for? Can we make what is often tacit into something more explicit?

What is meant by 'critique' and 'being critical'?

In the cultural context of a western university, it is both accepted and expected that academic enquiry will involve questioning the work and ideas of others, and students are often advised to be critical or at least to be 'more critical' by tutors. Anyone's work may be challenged and exposed to criticism. It is quite acceptable for students to question the ideas of leading academic figures in their area of study, as long as they can give convincing reasons for their view. But what exactly does the advice to be 'critical' mean?

54

The term 'critical' is widely used but rarely defined. The Oxford English Dictionary (OED) often provides a good starting point for a discussion. The Shorter OED uses terms such as 'involving or exercising careful judgement or observation'. It also includes the phrase 'given to judging', and the terms 'fault finding' and 'censorious'. The latter terms connect with the more negative aspects of being critical and its occasional use in everyday contexts when it relates to words such as 'judgemental', 'scathing' or the more vernacular 'nit-picking' – in these contexts to be critical can be seen as verging on being hostile, rude or confrontational.

My interpretation is closer to the first aspect of the above OED definition, that is, the notion that being critical involves the exercise of careful, deliberate and well-informed judgement. For example, in the literature review it is important for examiners to be sure that the student's critique is based on what is in the literature, and does not represent a misinterpretation or an ignorance of the literature.

We can present 'criticality' in terms of opposite poles, some of which relate to our actions and some to our dispositions or attitudes. Thus student criticality at doctoral level involves:

- Healthy scepticism … but not cynicism
- Confidence… but not 'cockiness' or arrogance
- Judgement which is critical…but not dismissive
- Opinions …without being opinionated
- Having a voice, taking a position … without 'sounding off'
- Being respectful … without being too humble
- Careful evaluation of published work … not serial shooting at random targets
- Being 'fair' by assessing cautiously the strengths and weaknesses of other people's ideas and writing … without prejudice
- Forming your own standpoint and values with respect to an argument, research project or publication … without getting up on a soap box
- Making judgements on the basis of considerable thought and all the available evidence – as opposed to assertions without reasons
- Putting forward recommendations and conclusions, whilst recognising their limitations … without being too apologetic or coy.

In summary: being critical is about having the confidence to make informed judgements. It is about students finding their own voice, their own values and building their own standpoint in the face of numerous other voices, from the literature and from other places. This is the quality, and one of the key

PRACTICAL ASPECTS OF THE EXAMINING PROCESS

criteria, that examiners should be looking for and commenting on in their independent reports.

WHERE DO THE INITIAL REPORTS GO AND WHEN CAN I SEE THE OTHER ONES?

In most cases, the internal and external will need to send their preliminary reports separately and independently to the research degrees office or the equivalent. They will be stored there and again in most cases the student will ultimately (usually after the recommendations have been made in the final report) be allowed to read them.

The examiners will not see the preliminary reports of the others until they have been submitted (to do this would be against regulations in every case that I am aware of). But, again, in most cases the examiners will share their reports when they meet for a pre-viva discussion. At this point it is very revealing (and to me quite adrenaline raising) to see what the other examiner(s) say in writing.

Preliminary reports, in my experience, rarely agree totally. However, there will often be some common ground – otherwise the process that follows can be difficult. Often, the initial reports will agree on the key criteria for the doctoral award – for example, that it has made a contribution. They tend to disagree on some (one hopes not many) of the criteria and qualities discussed above: for example, the level of criticality, the clarity of the writing, the use of literature or the methodology chosen. If the reports do disagree fundamentally, then a thorough and often robust discussion is needed prior to the viva – in cases where a Chair is present at this stage that can be very helpful.

It is often the case that the oral examination, the viva voce, can be of immense value in clearing up some of the disagreements between examiners. It is amazing, in my personal experience, that this happens so often and this is one of the reasons that I find the viva so useful and almost a therapeutic process.

HOW DOES THE WRITTEN THESIS 'SHAPE' THE VIVA?

One of the reasons suggested above that it is not the job of either examiner to make an exhaustive (and exhausting) list of typos in the initial report is that it could set the scene for a truly dreadful viva. I have seen this happen: one examiner wanted to proceed, page by page, with the student to point

56

out the errors – it became so tedious that I politely asked him to please stop. Although it is important that any doctoral dissertation should be as technically correct as possible before it 'goes public' electronically and as hard copy in the library, ensuring this 'technical correctness' is not the purpose of the viva.

We will discuss the viva and its purposes in the next chapter; but it is a statement of the obvious that the written submission will clearly shape the subsequent examination, whether the system requires viva or not. For example, if a thesis is not clearly written then the next stage of the examination will involve a large element of *clarification*. This may involve clarifying an argument or at more micro levels it may involve asking the student to make clear a paragraph or even a sentence. I have said before that my view is that every sentence in a dissertation should make sense. I have seen many submissions where this is simply not the case. This is often because the student has used either 'big words' in too liberal a way (a semantic problem) or perhaps words that do make sense but are put together in such a way as to be so turgid as to be incomprehensible.

Another influence that the written dissertation has on the examiners' subsequent work is that it may '*over claim*'. That is, its conclusions and recommendations may go well beyond its findings, its data. Incidentally, I have seen students 'under claim' and that may lead to other questions or suggestions for amendments later made by examiners. However, I would suggest that over claiming is more common – examiners will pick this up when reading and therefore it will be mentioned in their preliminary reports.

Finally, another example of how the written dissertation may affect subsequent examination and action by examiners is if it is guilty of '*over blame*'. I have seen this happen, particularly in professional doctorates, where students engage in some sort of blame-game at the end of their research. I have seen students blame everyone from managers, policy makers or even fellow practitioners or researchers for the situation that they have been researching. I must say that this is rare but it can be alarming for examiners when the final chapter is largely an exercise in blaming others. The above tendencies of over claiming and over blaming, where present, will shape the subsequent examination radically.

IN SUMMARY: SO THIS IS WHAT WE DO ... ?

I conclude this both chapter and the previous one on the practical aspects of examining, by considering what examiners actually do in practice. This section is based on a useful article published in 2014 and still highly relevant.

PRACTICAL ASPECTS OF THE EXAMINING PROCESS

It explored the business of 'What examiners actually do' when they assess a doctoral thesis (Golding et al. 2014). The three New Zealand authors did this by examining a range of literature and thereby looking at a variety of 'examiner practices'. The aim of the authors was to 'demystify the often secret process of assessing a thesis' – in many ways, the same as the key aim of this book. Here are the salient points:

1. Their first conclusion was that examiners 'tend to be broadly consistent in their practices and recommendations; they expect and want a thesis to pass, but first impressions are also very important'. I agree with the last two points: in my experience most examiners do hope that the student will succeed even if they have to give them extensive formative feedback to do so (see point 8). It is also the case, as discussed above, that the first impressions an examiner experiences when they open a thesis are crucial – and this is often the Abstract. As for the first point, it may be true that civil and competent examiners are 'broadly consistent' but I have witnessed (and had reported to me by students and colleagues) a number of examples of bad practice and inconsistency both in reading written submissions and in conducting the viva voce. I also know that although two (or more when this is the case) examiners of a doctorate do often agree and recommendations are arrived at painlessly, there are also instances when disagreement followed by lengthy debate occurs.

2. Examiners, and I would agree here, become 'annoyed and distracted by presentation errors', as discussed above.

3. Examiners look for work which forms a coherent whole – in my words, one which holds together.

4. They favour work which 'engages with the literature'.

5. Examiners also favour a thesis with a 'convincing approach' – my interpretation of this is that the writing is persuasive to the reader and has a 'thesis' in the sense of having an argument and a position.

6. Examiners look for a study which analyses and engages with its findings.

7. The authors suggest that examiners 'require a thesis to be publishable research'. My take on this is that publishability is a key criterion but it is fairer to students that examiners seek and explore elements of a doctoral thesis that are publishable (no thesis will be published in its entirety by a publisher unless the student goes for vanity publishing). Hartley's work on this aspect of doctoral studies is valuable here (see Chapters 6, 7 and 8).

58

8. The authors' last point is that examiners, as well as providing a final evaluation of a thesis, also give feedback and advice to students on how they can improve the thesis, how they can publish from it and how the research might be taken further. Again I fully agree with this observation and the sentiment behind it – it is the job of examiners to provide formative as well as summative feedback to doctoral students. This is good practice, although I have seen occasions where one examiner does not share this sentiment. Good examiners can and should advise students on how to improve their thesis before it becomes public and goes into a library (either electronically or on paper or both). This is another reason why, and another forum where, the face to face viva can be so valuable.

 FURTHER READING

The article explored in the last section is written by Clinton Golding, Sharon Sharmini and Ayelet Lazarovitch from the University of Otago, New Zealand, entitled: What Examiners actually do: what thesis students should know, in *Assessment & Evaluation in Higher Education*, 2014 Vol. 39, No. 5, 563–576.

One of the aspects that examiners tend to comment on in preliminary reports and then later explore in the viva is the literature review. For more detail see:

Holbrook, A. 2007. Levels of Success in the Use of the Literature in a Doctorate. *South African Journal of Higher Education* 21 (8): 1020–1041.

Holbrook, A., S. Bourke, H. Fairbairn, and T. Lovat. 2007. Examiner Comment on the Literature Review in PhD Theses. *Studies in Higher Education* 32 (3): 337–356.

Examiners' reports should include a mixture of formative and summative statements. The following articles examine in detail the style and substance of written reports and judgements on doctoral work:

Holbrook, A., S. Bourke, H. Fairbairn, and T. Lovat. 2012. The Focus and Substance of Formative Comment Provided by PhD Examiners. *Studies in Higher Education*: 1–18. doi:10.1080/03075079.2012.750289.

Holbrook, A., S. Bourke, T. Lovat, and K. Dally. 2004a. Qualities and Characteristics in the Written Reports of Doctoral Thesis Examiners. *Australian Journal of Educational and Developmental Psychology* 4: 126–152.

PRACTICAL ASPECTS OF THE EXAMINING PROCESS

Holbrook, A., S. Bourke, T. Lovat, and K. Dally. 2004b. PhD Theses at the Margin. *Melbourne Studies in Education* 45 (1): 89–115.

Holbrook, A., S. Bourke, T. Lovat, and K. Dally. 2004c. Investigating PhD Thesis Examination Reports. *International Journal of Educational Research* 41 (2): 98–120.

Holbrook, A., S. Bourke, T. Lovat, and H. Fairbairn. 2008. Consistency and Inconsistency in PhD Thesis Examination. *Australian Journal of Education* 52 (1): 36–48.

Johnston, S. 1997. Examining the Examiners: An Analysis of Examiners' Reports on Doctoral Theses. *Studies in Higher Education* 22 (3): 333–347.

Kemp, S., and C. McGuigan. 2009. Do PhD Examiners Agree on Their Recommendations? *New Zealand Journal of Education Studies* 44 (1): 47–57.

Kiley, M., and G. Mullins. 2004. Examining the Examiners: How Inexperienced Examiners Approach the Assessment of Research Theses. *International Journal of Educational Research* 41 (2): 121–135.

Kumar, V., and E. Stracke. 2011. Examiners' Reports on Theses: Feedback or Assessment? *Journal of English for Academic Purposes* 10 (4): 211–222. doi:10.1080/02602938.2013.798395.

Pearce, L. 2005. *How to examine a thesis*. Maidenhead: Open University Press.

For discussion of doctoral work in areas that do not require the 'traditional thesis' see:

Dally, K., A. Holbrook, A. Graham, and M. Lawry. 2004. The Processes and Parameters of Fine Art PhD Examination. *International Journal of Educational Research* 41 (2): 136–162.

Winter, R., M. Griffith, and K. Green. 2000. The Academic Qualities of Practice. *Studies in Higher Education* 25 (1): 25–37.

WEBSITES

For a superb summary of the practical and theoretical aspects of being critical I have seen nothing better than Jenny Moon's discussion, neatly entitled 'We seek it here … .a new perspective on the activity of critical thinking' (the title has a nod to The Kinks if I remember their song correctly). This discussion is of great value to doctoral examiners.

http://escalate.ac.uk/downloads/2041.pdf

(accessed 19/02/2020)

Part III

Judgements, decisions and their aftermath

Chapter 6

Making the decision

SOURCES OF DEBATE AND THE NEED TO REACH AGREEMENT

When it comes to the examiners making their decisions and the writing of the final report there is considerable room for debate and disagreement (or, as Tinkler and Jackson (2000) put it, 'confusion'!). The first source of debate is that procedures vary to some degree (not totally) in at least three ways: from one university to another, across disciplines and from one examiner to another, depending on their background and experience. Thus, although criteria for the doctoral award are written down in the regulations which are given to examiners, they do vary between universities; worse than this, I have known at least one examiner who has not read them, several who have just 'skimmed' them, and a few others who have simply assumed they will be the same as their own university. This is a risky assumption.

On top of the variation in written criteria for doctoral awards, there are also huge differences in the way that these criteria are interpreted by different examiners. This is why the examination of the doctorate is unique among assessment practices in Higher Education or indeed education at any level: those making the judgement have a large level of autonomy and freedom. There are no set, agreed learning objectives as there are in undergraduate programmes for example. Then there is the leeway, as one might call it, when individuals interpret written statements. The most common words and criteria that are wide open to interpretation are:

- Critical/criticality: we discussed this at length earlier but one examiner's view that the student is being 'adequately critical' may not accord with the view of the other(s).

63

- Originality: again, this was discussed earlier. It has a wide range of interpretations and these will vary from one person to another.
- Publishability: one examiner, perhaps if she/he is the editor of a journal, may have a clear idea of what is publishable in her/his own journal. This may be totally different for another editor or reviewer for another journal. One person's favoured journal, style and contents may be another's poison.

Other words are often thrown into the discussion by examiners whilst 'thrashing out' their decision; some of these words are not even in the written regulations in my experience. Descriptions or criteria such as 'engaging' are used; this is a good quality to have in a thesis but is often not in written regulations. Another that I have heard is that 'it is not rigorous or robust enough' – again, I have seen these thrown into discussion and yet not seen them in that particular university's written criteria; and the words 'rigorous' and 'robust' have almost as many interpretations as there are examiners.

THE EXAMINERS: INTERNAL AND EXTERNAL(S)

In some ways the jobs of the two (or sometimes three) examiners are the same. They are all there to conduct a thorough and fair assessment of a doctoral submission which they have previously read. They will all have written a preliminary report in advance (often only one week prior) and this should include some indications of how the viva will be conducted (see Chapter 5).

An important chemistry: the relative status, interaction and roles of the two examiners

In my view the weight of all examiners should be equal, regardless of their experience, standing in the field, or whether they are internal to the department or external. In practice, and this happens despite documents and guidelines to the contrary, I have often seen tacit (and sometimes explicit) acceptance between examiners that one carries more influence than another. How does this show itself? I have experienced the following: one person saying that they are not an expert in the field and actually stating that they did not know why they had been asked to be an examiner; one examiner being deferent to another by 'agreeing' to their judgement rather than standing their ground; one examiner assuming superiority over the others, perhaps by (as they say) 'pulling rank' or citing greater experience.

MAKING THE DECISION

None of these behaviours is either justified or documented. It often pans out in the viva itself where one examiner dominates the questioning and will not give way to the other(s). It sometimes shows itself in the discussion, agreement on, and then the writing of the final report and recommendations. Equal weight should be observed but this is not always the case. I have seen less experienced examiners 'bow down' to the views and judgements of another who is deemed to be of more 'authority' or standing. Where a Chair is present at a viva, as we consider later (see Chapter 7), then he or she can ensure that none of these unwanted and unprofessional human interactions will occur.

POSSIBLE OUTCOMES AND NAMES FOR THEM

Roughly speaking, examiners can make the following recommendations. I say 'roughly speaking' because every university has a slightly different way of phrasing these and often different time periods for the recommended work to be carried out. Hence, it is vital that each examiner (internal and external) should check the fine print of the regulations. The main categories that examiners can recommend in their final report are:

- Pass with no corrections
- Pass, subject to the completion of specified minor amendment (within a specified timescale)
- Major amendments: I have seen these described as 'less minor' or 'less straightforward' amendments (this is the grey area discussed below)
- Referral or resubmission
- Where there is a viva, resubmission with the requirement of a second viva
- The recommendation that a dissertation submitted for a PhD should be awarded an MPhil
- Fail.

I have now examined roughly 100 doctorates (most with a viva involved) and there are three of these bullet points that I have never seen recommended in the joint report. The first of these is 'Pass with no corrections'. Call me a grumpy old 'so and so' (I have heard worse) but I cannot see how a lengthy doctoral dissertation of over 70,000 words with a Reference list of several pages can ever be perfect. I have seen many superb dissertations but I have

65

never seen a perfect one. If two or more examiners have been over the written thesis with a fine toothcomb, then they will find things that can be changed, corrected or improved upon. These may be typos. There might be one or two sentences that could be improved; there may be references that are incomplete or even literature that should have been included but was not. All these improvements would be classed as minor amendments or corrections. Asking for these shows that the examiners treat doctoral assessment as a *formative* event as well as a summative one. It also shows that they have taken the time to read the dissertation carefully.

The second reason why the 'straight pass' recommendation is rarely made (as I said, never in my experience) is due to the viva voce. In an engaging, active, challenging viva an issue will always arise, or the student may say something new or extremely insightful. At that moment, and I have seen this happen many times, in the intensity of the oral, the examiners may think: 'that is an excellent point – but is it in the written thesis?' I have even seen (if one can see thought) the student and perhaps her supervisor (if present) have this same realisation during the viva. It will certainly be a talking point in the post viva session and again can result in minor amendments which will improve the thesis before it goes into the library in print or as an e-resource. This is discussed at length in Chapter 7.

The two other bullet points that I have never seen recommended by examiners in doctoral judgements that I have been involved in are the last two: the award of an MPhil and the judgement of Fail. I am sure that they have occurred in the history of examining but I have never witnessed these recommendations over a thirty year period as examiner or supervisor. This is largely due to my own, personal views of the doctoral examining process, i.e. I feel that the examiners and the supervisors have let the student down if either of these last two are 'ticked' on the final report. If it is not yet 'ready' for a PhD or a PD then perhaps the student and supervisor should not have submitted it. If the examiners read a dissertation in that category then their job, indeed their responsibility, is to suggest to the student and supervisor exactly what needs to be done to raise it to the required standard. Their role then is a truly formative one and this points to the recommendation of 're-submission' (or the equivalent in that university's terminology).

BORDER ISSUES: DISCUSSING THE GREY AREAS

Normally, at least in my experience, the grey areas are at two boundaries: the first is the decision of whether to suggest minor amendments or more major changes. The second is between major amendments or referral/

MAKING THE DECISION

resubmission. Other areas sometimes need discussion, such as the decision on whether a second viva is necessary, but these occur less frequently.

Let's start with minor amendments or 'corrections'. These may be extremely minor, even to the point of being pedantic – but one small part of the examiner's job is to be pedantic! Thus the correction of 'typos' is a necessary requirement – why would or should examiners allow a written dissertation to go public if it has typographical errors in it? For me this includes: missing or mis-used apostrophes (such as the confusion of 's for s'); incorrect plurals such as phenomena for phenomenon or criteria for criterion, and references which are incomplete or even missing. It is very difficult, in over seventy thousand words, not to make these mistakes and there may well be some in this book; although as a book author I have the huge advantage of a copy editor. But I would be disappointed if a reader or a copy editor did not point these out to me.

Incidentally, there are certain other tendencies in students' writing which annoy me slightly, e.g. saying 'data is' rather than 'data are', and saying that 'x impacted y' rather than impacted 'on' or 'upon', but I have learnt to live with these.

Some universities provide reasonably (not totally) clear advice on what constitutes 'minor amendments'. For example, I recently found these statements from Birmingham City University (BCU) helpful whilst external examining there:

> Minor amendments should be corrections or changes which the examiners feel would improve the presentation of the thesis and would include for example correction of typographical, spelling or stylistic errors, slight reordering of, but not significant amendment to, content; amendments to the abstract; changes which are intended to provide clarification.

In common with most universities they state that minor amendments should not involve significant rewriting or changes to the way research outcomes are presented. Minor amendments do *not* include collection of more data, any further research or reanalysis of existing data. In most cases, if further research and analysis is needed and the extra work required can be described as 'substantive', this would lead to a recommendation of 'Resubmission'. There are often two rather grey areas, in my view, between (firstly) minor and major amendments and (secondly) major amendments and resubmission. BCU, for example, state that 'major amendments should be corrections

67

or changes to improve the content, analysis or clarification but when the originality of the central thesis is recognised'. They can involve rewriting or significant changes to the way research outcomes are presented. In some ways then, the distinction between minor and major is a matter of degree. It seems to me that the key distinction between major amendments and resubmission is the necessity (in the latter) to undertake further research.

You can see from this short discussion that, even when regulations are carefully stated, as in the BCU examples above, there will inevitably be discussion over the borders between minor, major and resubmission. It is vital that examiners do study regulations carefully but that will certainly not pre-empt or prevent debate over the final recommendation to be made in the joint report.

Of course, the final recommendation made is of both vital importance and practical significance to the student. If minor amendments are asked for, these will normally need to be completed within (usually) six weeks of the formal notification sent to the student. If the amendments are major, then the student will often be given six months to make them. If a resubmission is asked for, then the time period is often twelve months (and perhaps with a second viva). In some universities this may involve the student paying an additional fee.

Examiners will normally reach an agreement and indeed they have a responsibility to do so. Most universities make provision for a situation where examiners' recommendations are not unanimous. This may involve accepting the judgement of the external examiner; it might involve a majority recommendation or very occasionally the appointment of an additional external examiner. Once again, these possibilities should be fully covered in the stated regulations.

POST JUDGEMENT

The work of the examiners does not end at the point of the initial, agreed judgement. If minor amendments are to be made then a decision needs to be made on how these will be checked and who will be responsible for the checking process. Where the student (PhD or Prof Doc) is a member of staff at the university, then two externals will need to be involved in the initial assessment, sometimes with the addition of an internal. Then the examiners will need to decide on who will make the final check.

It is vital that the examiners have a clear agreement on this. Then, the actual amendments, plus an agreed procedure on how they should be done,

68

are conveyed to both student and supervisor. With minor amendments, it may well be the internal examiner who takes (or has to take) responsibility for this. She or he should then tell the student how this should be done. My own favoured approach is for the student (with the help of the supervisor) to email these to the allocated examiner, showing clearly which correction they are addressing, where it occurs and what change has been made. This is far preferable to the student emailing an entire thesis and the examiner being left to work through it to check every change.

Similar procedures and decisions will apply if 'more major' or 'less straightforward' amendments are asked for. On the other hand, if the decision is 'referral' or 'resubmission' then in some ways the whole examination process starts from the beginning. It may or may not result in a second viva (this has only happened to me once).

The 'aftermath' of the initial examination process is examined in more detail in Chapters 7 and 8.

THE VIVA

In many countries (not all) the final decision will be made following an oral examination of the student: the viva voce or live voice. In this case, the viva is an important and integral part of the doctoral examination. It is neither some sort of 'add-on' nor an opportunity to meet the student for a 'cosy chat'. I have heard all of these descriptions used, wrongly, by examiners and sometimes supervisors. The viva is a part of the examination process – therefore it is against regulations for anyone to say at the beginning of the oral that 'you have passed but we just need to check a few things with you'. Again, I have heard this said (or been told this in pre-viva meetings by the other examiner); this is not only wrong, it is against regulations. We fully consider the purpose and conduct of the viva in the next chapter.

 FURTHER READING

For other discussions of how 'quality' is assessed and how examiners reach agreement (or do not!) in doctoral examining see:

Bourke, S. 2007. PhD Thesis Quality. *South African Journal of Higher Education* 21 (8): 1042–1052.

Bourke, S., J. Hattie, and L. Anderson. 2004. Predicting Examiner Recommendations on PhD Theses. *International Journal of Educational Research* 41 (2): 178–194.

JUDGEMENTS, DECISIONS AND THEIR AFTERMATH

Carter, S. 2008. Examining the Doctoral Thesis. *Innovations in Education and Teaching International* 45 (4): 365–374.

Denicolo, P. 2003. Assessing the PhD. *Quality Assurance in Education* 11 (2): 84–91.

Holbrook, A., S. Bourke, T. Lovat, and K. Dally. 2004a. Qualities and Characteristics in the Written Reports of Doctoral Thesis Examiners. *Australian Journal of Educational and Developmental Psychology* 4: 126–152.

Holbrook, A., S. Bourke, T. Lovat, and K. Dally. 2004b. PhD Theses at the Margin. *Melbourne Studies in Education* 45 (1): 89–115.

Holbrook, A., S. Bourke, T. Lovat, and K. Dally. 2004c. Investigating PhD Thesis Examination Reports. *International Journal of Educational Research* 41 (2): 98–120.

Holbrook, A., S. Bourke, T. Lovat, and H. Fairbairn. 2008. Consistency and Inconsistency in PhD Thesis Examination. *Australian Journal of Education* 52 (1): 36–48.

Kemp, S., and C. McGuigan. 2009. Do PhD Examiners Agree on Their Recommendations? *New Zealand Journal of Education Studies* 44 (1): 47–57.

Kiley, M., and G. Mullins. 2004. Examining the Examiners: How Inexperienced Examiners Approach the Assessment of Research Theses. *International Journal of Educational Research* 41 (2): 121–135.

Pearce, L. 2005. *How to examine a thesis*. Maidenhead: Open University Press.

Chapter 7

The oral examination (live voice)
Why, what and how

WHY DO WE HAVE VIVAS?

Written regulations from universities should state the purpose of the viva. Common statements include: to test the candidate's knowledge of his/her research and subject area; to allow examiners to clarify any queries that may have arisen when reading the thesis; to judge whether the candidate has developed research skills appropriate to doctoral level; to give the candidate the opportunity to 'defend' the thesis in person; to establish whether candidates fully understand the implications of their work. Some university regulations state explicitly that one of the main purposes is to ascertain whether the work is the candidate's own.

Many regulations inform us (that is: the student, the supervisor and the examiners) that the viva is an integral part of the examination of the degree – in other words, the oral is actually part of the examining process, not (say) a confirmation of any predetermined judgement. It is not a rubber-stamping exercise. Students, supervisors and examiners perhaps need to remind themselves of this – the examination as a whole involves more than just a judgement of the written work, i.e. the written and oral elements of the examination for a doctorate complement each other. For many universities, the written thesis is only 'part fulfilment' of the requirements for a doctorate.

From a more negative perspective, if a thesis does not meet the necessary criteria, some university regulations state that one purpose of the oral is to ascertain reasons why a student's work is *not* deemed to attain doctoral standard. This might lead to questions about supervision, research training, resources or any mitigating personal circumstances.

As we have seen, some countries do not have a viva and often this may be for geographical reasons rather than academic ones. My view is that distance can be overcome by using the technology now widely available for

71

conducting a viva via 'remote attendance'. I have conducted several vivas using modern video link techniques and older technology such as Skype. These have been almost, not quite, as useful and enjoyable as an oral discussion in the same room. In my view, the direct, human discussion in the viva is an important and valuable part of the doctoral examining process. Not only is it a huge event for the student (and the supervisor) it is an equally important occasion for the examiners.

In summary for this first section, the purposes of the viva are:

- Authentication: is the research the student's own work?
- Clarification and explanation: of ideas, interpretations, and conclusions – or even specific sentences
- Justification: why did you do it this way and not that way? Why did you interpret your data in the way you did?
- Location: how does your research sit in relation to the wider field?
- Exploration, elaboration and development: how can these ideas/analyses/methods be taken further and developed?
- Publication and projection: which elements can be taken forward for publication and where? What further research does the thesis suggest or point to?
- Reflection and evaluation: on the process and the product of the research
- Narration: telling the story of what was done, how and why.

PRIVATE VERSUS PUBLIC?

In the UK, the viva is held in a suitable room with those present being (at most) the examiners, student, supervisor(s) and the Chair. In other countries, such as Finland and Sweden, the viva is a public affair held in a large room such as a lecture theatre, and is open to everyone from the student's family and friends to the person in the street who fancies seeing a good ceremony. It is sometimes called a 'public defense'. Some see this model as preferable to the 'behind closed doors' version. The public approach is transparent in that everyone or anyone can witness it, the student often has to stand up and offer a 'defense' of their work, and the examiners are invited to ask questions at the end of this public statement. All is clear and above board. The result is a ceremony and a ritual, often followed by further rituals and congratulations.

In reality, and I am sorry to sound opinionated, I find the public version to be little more than a ceremony or rite of passage. In most cases the student knows in advance if she or he has passed. The first public viva I did was in Finland: I was asked by email, after I had read the dissertation, but before I travelled over, if they 'could arrange a celebration and a party, followed by a joint sauna' after the event. I said yes. I was measured up for a suit of clothes rather like a tuxedo; when I arrived they asked if I had any shiny, patent leather shoes. I did not, so the evening before they found me a pair in my size. It was a thoroughly enjoyable affair. I was able to ask a limited number of fairly bland questions to the student; the celebrations afterwards were unforgettable. Was it a rigorous test of the student's research, reading and understanding? Certainly not. Was it part of the examination process? No.

STUDENTS' PERSPECTIVES ON THE VIVA

This section comes early in this long chapter because I feel that examiners need to be aware of the student perspective when they prepare for and begin the viva. It is important for examiners to take into account the student's perceptions, anticipations and emotional reactions to the viva experience. Many doctoral students, especially those doing PDs, will be experienced at presenting orally during their own working lives. But for everyone, presenting in the viva situation is likely to be a new experience and to offer a new challenge. For every doctoral candidate the oral examination is an important matter. For some it is a cause of anxiety and concern. It is not always a positive experience for the student, as discussed shortly.

Have students been supported in preparing for their viva?

Examiners can tell within seconds whether a student has been prepared for the oral examination. The two unwanted extremes can be: either the student has over rehearsed (see later in this chapter); or he or she shows complete shock that examiners are asking them difficult questions about work which these new faces should have read before the meeting! I have even had a student in a viva telling me as an examiner, after I had posed a question about a section of the dissertation, that 'it's all in the text, on pages x to y' and then turning to those pages. This is not a good way to endear the examiner!

As for being 'over rehearsed', mock vivas are considered by some departments to be highly advisable and even obligatory in some HEIs. I have mixed feelings on this. There is a danger that they somehow steal the thunder or remove the spontaneity from the final viva; there is probably a larger danger that the mock viva bears absolutely no resemblance to either the content or the conduct of the actual event (both discussed later in this chapter). To me the main positive aspect of the mock viva is that it may help to develop the student's spoken skill and offer practice in answering difficult questions orally with the pressure of faces to face.

Students' views of and experiences of the viva

Examiners should be aware that a number of interesting, if occasionally worrying, studies have been conducted on the student's view of the viva. The focus has been largely on the PhD experience rather than the professional doctorate. Prior to the viva, most studies unsurprisingly report that students vary from being confident to anxious to extremely anxious (Hartley and Jory 2000), in some cases saying they feel 'sick' or 'terrified'. Following the viva, reported student experiences vary (predictably) according to the outcome. Thus the successful students in Hartley and Jory's study of psychology graduates (the passers) were most likely to report a boost in their morale and self-esteem, although one passer felt that his self-esteem had been reduced. The majority, whether passing or otherwise, seemed to find the experience 'draining'. The time allotted to the visas experienced in this study ranged from a rather short 45 minutes to a ridiculous 4.25 hours. The vast majority of the students surveyed felt that the viva had been fair, especially the passers. In response to an open question about ideas for improvement to the viva, a significant number suggested the need for standardisation (e.g. on length and guidelines) and less variability. Later research by Jackson and Tinkler (2001) reported more negative experiences than Hartley and Jory, even amongst the passers. Some of the responses spoke of 'misery and humiliation, harassment and suffering' (Jackson and Tinkler 2001: 362). From 88 respondents, 20% described the tone of their viva as 'hostile', 'sarcastic' or 'insulting' – although 60% were more positive using adjectives such as 'relaxed', 'friendly' and 'enjoyable'. One of the interesting points to note is that an important number of candidates reported that their perceptions of 'academic competence' had decreased as a result of the viva, as had their desire to work within academia (even one tenth of the passers expressed this negative view).

WHO WILL BE IN THE ROOM? CAN (OR SHOULD) SUPERVISORS ATTEND?

One of the questions that students rightly ask – and I sometimes wonder myself when I travel to a new venue for a viva – is the question of who will be there.

THE ORAL EXAMINATION (LIVE VOICE)

Firstly, and most importantly, there should never be an elephant in the room.

In some universities, the external examiner will be expected and invited to chair the oral. In many, there is now an 'independent chair' whose role is partly to check that procedures are followed correctly. In some cases the supervisor(s) may be present at the oral – but they should certainly not play a part in the actual discussion. My own view is that the student should confer with supervisors on their presence and make the request for the supervisors to be present between them. For example, one student might feel that the supervisor's presence could give them support and confidence. A supervisor's presence may also be valuable when it comes to making notes, especially if revisions are ultimately required. However, another might feel that the supervisor could be a distraction or an impediment to a full discussion. In all cases, if the supervisor is present, eye contact between student and supervisor is best avoided (a suitable arrangement of chairs could ensure this).

In practice, supervisors often attend the viva, and in some HEIs it is compulsory to do so. I have conducted vivas where the student had three supervisors and they have all shown up! Since the supervisor is not allowed to speak at all during a viva, it is also best if the supervisor is out of sight (but still able to listen) and therefore out of mind. I once acted as an external for the PhD of an overseas student whose English was good but rather hesitant (which one should expect and deal with as an examiner by giving the student time). The supervisor was present and for the first two questions – which the nervous student answered slowly but surely – the supervisor said to both responses 'What she means to say is …' . After the second interruption we asked him to leave the room – our 'red card' was not well received but from then on the student gained confidence, stopped looking at her supervisor for reassurance and produced an excellent oral experience.

The presence of the supervisor can also be off-putting for the examiners. This can be particularly true if the supervisor is of a 'higher status' than one or more examiners (either internal or external), if they have past connections (good or bad), or if their body language is distracting. Hence the golden rule: out of sight out of mind!

In summary, there are pluses and minuses to the supervisor being present. On the plus side, they can listen, make notes, provide feedback later, and during the viva may be seen as support or reassurance for the student. On the negative side, they may be distracting to the student or examiners, they may alter the dynamics of the occasion, and they can put extra

75

pressure on the student. My personal view is that it should be the student's choice whether her supervisor(s) is present at the viva. They can discuss it in advance and make a careful decision prior to what is a once-in-a-lifetime event. As a supervisor I have always asked my students whether they want me to be present or not. Many do but I had one who thought carefully about it and finally said, 'Sorry, I'd rather you weren't there'. After drying my tears I asked why; she made two points: one, that she might keep looking round for me for reassurance; and two, that it was 'her' occasion. (Mine too, I thought, but I kept it to myself.)

THE FIRST ENCOUNTER...

In every viva that I have done (as internal or examiner) I have encountered not only a different student (an obvious point) but also a different approach and attitude. No two students are the same. Perhaps the only emotion or attitude that I see most commonly is that the student is nervous at the beginning – and understandably so. A big event is coming.

Students seem to vary somewhere along a continuum from terrified to overly confident and even arrogant. A passage from a novel by Sally Rooney in 2018 (*Normal People*) sums up the latter category of student perfectly. She is talking about a working class boy's realisation when he goes to a top university (Trinity College Dublin) that he is not as 'thick' as he is perceived to be, or thinks he is:

> This is what it's like in Dublin. All Connell's classmates have identical accents and carry the same MacBook under their arms. In seminars they express their opinions passionately and conduct impromptu debates. Unable to form such straightforward views or express them with any force, Connell usually felt a sense of crushing inferiority … as if he had upgraded himself accidentally to an intellectual level far above his own … He did gradually start to wonder why all their classroom discussions were so abstract and lacking in actual detail, and eventually he realised that most people were not actually doing the reading. They were coming into College every day to have heated debates about books they had not read. He understands now that his classmates are not like him. It's easy for them to have opinions and express them with confidence. They don't worry about appearing ignorant or conceited. They are not stupid people but they're not so much smarter than him either. They just move through the world

THE ORAL EXAMINATION (LIVE VOICE)

in a different way, and he'll probably never understand them, and he thinks they will never understand him, or even try.

(Rooney 2018, 67–68)

This is a brilliant passage for its observation of the two extremes that an examiner is likely to meet. Connell is diffident, unsure of himself, embarrassed by his accent and has feelings akin to the impostor syndrome. (He reminds me of myself as a shy 17 year old on my first day at Bristol University when I met some very pleasant public schoolboys from Harrow who thought that my local, West Country accent was American.) In reality, it turns out that Connell is more able than most of his classmates and is eventually offered a postgraduate scholarship in the USA. Examiners will meet the Connell type, who may be nervous at the start, slightly unsure and wondering what they are doing there in trying to gain a PhD. Examiners need to be prepared for this self-perception and deal with it in a sympathetic way, without ever being patronising. This approach will lead to a constructive, enjoyable viva.

In contrast, examiners may meet the type of student that Connell has seen through. They may be over confident to the point of being arrogant – they may not have read deeply even if they seem to have read widely. They will answer with great assurance and apparent authority. This is why it is important for examiners to ask for examples – only by hearing a good example of an abstract idea or concept can an examiner be satisfied that a student fully understands it. It is important that, unlike Connell's classmates, a student during a viva should not be allowed to talk in generalities and abstractions for too long. Detail must be sought; examples should be asked for.

Of course, the paragraphs above really portray caricatures or extremes. In practice, one meets a student somewhere along the spectrum between Connell and the MacBook carriers at the opposite pole.

CONDUCTING THE VIVA VOCE

Normally, the oral examination, or viva, should be arranged within a set time period from receipt of the thesis by the examiners. This might be ten weeks or even twelve weeks – regulations should be checked for this. The internal examiner or the supervisor (regulations vary) will have responsibility for arranging the date of the oral with the external – this date should then be confirmed with the student, at the very least two weeks prior to the suggested date. A suitable venue is arranged, usually on the campus of the awarding university.

We have seen that both examiners should complete a preliminary report on the thesis independently and then arrange to confer prior to the oral. This liaison, or meeting, should be used to exchange and discuss preliminary reports (these reports are not seen by the student or supervisor). The two examiners should also decide on the procedure and content of the viva, i.e. what will be asked, who will be asking what and in what order. A good oral should have some sort of structure with prearranged questions and issues, and a predetermined order. However, an oral should be viewed rather like a semi-structured interview – the discussion, if it is a good one, may lead on to other questions and sub-questions, and deviate from the plan (see later in this chapter).

We discuss the actual content and behaviour of the examiners during the viva in detail later, by looking at good practice and bad. This short section ends with a useful quote from the regulations of the University of Leicester:

The viva exam should be a positive experience for the research student and should be conducted in a fair, transparent, and professional manner. The research student should be put at their ease as far as possible during the exam. If an examination chair is present they will be expected to write a short report on the conduct of the exam and this should be appended to the examiners' joint report paperwork.

Conducting the viva for the professional doctorate

Just two brief points to note here: first, there is a high probability that the examiners and supervisors of doctorates (whether professional or otherwise) do not themselves have a professional doctorate. Examiners have a duty to be fully aware of the PD, its aims and its regulations. The second, related to the first, is that one of the features in the assessment of a professional doctorate as opposed to a traditional PhD relates to the discussion earlier in this book, on the nature of different doctorates. The PD can be seen (rather glibly) as producing 'researching professionals', with the PhD aiming to prepare 'professional researchers' and some sort of entry or initiation into academia following 'live' peer review. These different conceptions should be reflected in the viva in the different contexts, though in reality this may not always happen and the actual student viva experience will depend (as always) on the two examiners and the way they work together.

78

THE CONTENT OF A VIVA VOCE

The 'content' of an oral examination will inevitably vary from one thesis to another, one field to another and between disciplines. However, there are certain general procedures for 'good practice' that are likely to be followed and indeed many University regulations insist that they are followed.

Good practice

Students should expect certain aspects of 'good practice' to be followed for the viva, although reality may fall short in some respects. The responsibility for ensuring good practice should fall on both the internal and external examiners. The venue for the viva may be someone's office or it could be a seminar or meeting room. The room for the viva should be suitably laid out with seating organised so that eye contact can be made between student and examiners (if the supervisor is present, he or she should literally take more of a back seat). The viva should start with polite introductions all round, led by the external if he or she is the Chair. The Chair should explain what the viva is for, i.e. a focused discussion (not an interrogation) with others who know the field, which gives the student a chance to bring their thesis 'to life'. Most regulations do not permit examiners to tell students whether they have passed or failed at the start of the viva – this seems perfectly logical given that the viva is an integral part of the examination. No specific recommendations (regarding pass, fail, minor amendments, and resubmission) should be made at all during the course of the viva – they should be conveyed clearly after the examiners have conferred after the viva has finished. However, it seems civilised, and conducive to a good discussion, to put the student at ease with a comment such as 'we have enjoyed reading your thesis; we found it very interesting and it raises some important issues'.

For most candidates, this will be their first viva (and possibly the last) so examiners should explain the process and procedures to them (in brief) – again with the aim of making them less nervous. It would seem to be good practice to start with a relatively easy, 'warm-up' question: 'tell us in brief what your thesis is about'; 'why did you choose this topic to research?' 'What surprised you most in doing this study?' Specific questions will then follow, not all of which should have been pre-planned.

JUDGEMENTS, DECISIONS AND THEIR AFTERMATH

General questions that might be asked in a doctoral viva

It is impossible to predict the exact questions, especially the highly specific ones that will be asked in a viva. This depends on the written thesis, the preliminary reports and the interactions in the room between all parties. However, from my observations of around one hundred vivas I have compiled a list below of the very *general* questions that tend to come up in the viva. I now use it as a checklist for my own external examining:

1. Motivation: What made you do this piece of research? Why do think it is important?
2. Position: What is your own position (professional or personal) in relation to this field and these research questions? What prior conceptions and/or experiences did you bring to this study? How did these influence your data analysis and data collection?
3. Research questions: What were the main research questions that you were trying to address in your work? What was the origin of these questions?
4. Literature review: What shaped or guided your literature review? Why did it cover the areas that it did (and not others)? Why did you/didn't you include the work of X in your study?
5. Methodology: Why did you employ the methods you used? Why not others, e.g. X? What informed your choice of methods? What would you do differently, with hindsight?
6. Data analysis: Did anything surprise you in the data ('hit you in the face')? Any anomalies?
7. Further work: Which aspects of the work could be taken further? How?
8. Contribution: Please could you summarise your thesis? What are the main findings of your research? What did you learn from doing it? What original contribution to knowledge do you feel that you have made? What are its key messages?
9. Publication: Which elements of your work do you feel are worthy of publication and/or presentation at a conference? What plans do you have for publication and dissemination?
10. Reflections: What are the strengths of your thesis? And its limitations or weaknesses?

Incidentally, these are exactly the same questions that student and supervisor should ask of the written thesis before it is submitted. A good written

THE ORAL EXAMINATION (LIVE VOICE)

dissertation should consider and address all of the ten questions above before it is presented for examination.

GOOD PRACTICE IN ASKING QUESTIONS

The importance of actually asking questions

The main purpose of the viva is to ask the student questions, indeed quite a lot of questions. It also serves the purpose of allowing the student to bring her thesis to life, to make it more than just words on paper, and to show enthusiasm and passion. It is, as one of my students said to me, 'a chance to shine'.

So the examiners' job is to ask questions. They are not there to show off, demonstrate how clever they are, or to engage in long monologues. I once acted as internal for a PhD student and the external examiner was long-winded, to put it mildly. During the viva, after he had spoken for perhaps two minutes (that is a long monologue) I had to say to him: 'please can you tell me what your question is?' I had lost track of his line of probing, so had the student … and even the external seemed to have lost focus in those two minutes.

Questions to avoid

Given that questioning the student about their thesis is the examiners' main role (and the *raison d'être* of the viva) then it is worth considering what counts as a 'good question' and what a bad question is. I have listed below seven categories of question which should always be avoided during the oral examination:

1. Hypothetical questions: 'if you had been the leader of X, what would you have done?'
2. Leading questions: 'I hate the work of X, so why did you even consider it?'
3. 'Clever' questions to show off your superior knowledge: 'are you more drawn to Wittgenstein's earlier thinking or to his later philosophy?' or 'have you read the research that I did in 1993?'
4. Compound questions, either double barrelled, triple or worse.
5. Emotive or obviously biased questions, as in point 2 above: 'I have always hated the work of X – why on earth did you use his work?'
6. Questions that are impossible to answer, of the ilk: 'why do horses have four legs?'

81

JUDGEMENTS, DECISIONS AND THEIR AFTERMATH

7. Ambiguous, confusing, unclear, long-winded, imprecise or overgeneral questions.

These are all categories of question that I have seen or rather heard during a doctoral viva. There may well be more types of question that are examples of bad practice so I would welcome responses from readers if they have been subjected to, or have heard, others.

What is 'good questioning'?

The list above shows my own take on bad questions: so my simple answer to 'what is a good question?' is to say, well, the opposite, or at least the avoidance, of the categories above. But I also feel that one way to test if a student has really understood something is to ask them to give an example. I think it was Wittgenstein (though perhaps Einstein, but certainly not Rick Stein) who said something like: to show that someone really understands something they should be able to give an example of it, i.e. the best way to show understanding of an abstract notion or a theory is to give a concrete instance of it: to bring concrete to abstract. Asking for this is often the best way of probing – it is also very demanding so examiners should be patient when waiting for a good response. Examiners need to be good listeners.

In summary for this section, the job of the examiners is to pose questions directly to the student: these may ask for clarification, explanation, elaboration, justification or exemplification. Most of the time of the viva should be taken up by the student's responses – not by the over lengthy questions, or, even worse, long monologues, from examiners.

Some university regulations now give general guidance on good practice in asking questions. I have adapted and paraphrased the bullet points below from handbooks that I have been provided with as an external examiner. Examiners should:

- Ask questions in a constructive and positive way, as opposed to being negative or aggressive, e.g. 'why did you use method X?' as opposed to 'what came over you when you decided to do Y?'
- Use a range of questioning techniques: closed and open; specific and general
- Give students time to formulate and reflect before they answer and encourage them to do this
- Praise good answers, i.e. if they are insightful, incisive or help to clarify an issue or argument in the thesis

82

THE ORAL EXAMINATION (LIVE VOICE)

- Allow candidates the opportunity to recover from a poor answer that may be a result of nerves or misunderstanding. Examiners should rephrase a question and pose it in a different way, thus helping not only to clarify it but also to allow the student some recovery time.

Some of these points are particularly important when English is an additional language for the student. The candidate may be far more adept with written English than with oral situations. The onus is on examiners to speak clearly, to pose questions that are brief, clear and actually make sense, and to give students time to answer – indeed, this is good practice whatever the student's first language.

Beware of your idioms

Finally, examiners should avoid the use of idioms during or after the viva. This applies to all students, not just international postgraduates. During supervision, I regularly used the expression 'horses for courses' in discussing the choice of appropriate methods until a home student told me that he did not know what I meant. This experience has made me aware of the dangers of idioms ever since.

Just to be tongue-in-cheek for a second, I have heard or seen all of the following used during doctoral examining:

The bottom line is that you can't see the wood for the trees; with a bit of jiggery-pokery this thesis could cut the mustard; once you see daylight and let the dog see the rabbit, then it should be a case of 'Bob's your Uncle'. You were on the right track but a few red herrings and flies in the ointment led you to make a mountain out of a molehill.

What? A strange kettle of fish but I have seen it happen, no kidding. I don't want to make a meal of it but for students idioms may be the last straw in pulling the wool over their eyes. So bite the bullet, go the whole hog, and give them the chop.

BAD PRACTICE AND STRANGE BEHAVIOUR IN THE CONDUCT OF VIVAS

I have personally witnessed, and heard many rumours about, some of the poor practice and unusual behaviours that can take place in an oral examination. Fortunately, my estimate is that these happen more and more rarely.

83

Some examiners seem to arrive with a bee, or several bees, in their bonnets (please pardon the idiom). They have rigid views on what or whose writing should be included in a thesis. Very often, such people will expect the student to have cited this examiner's own work or to have read their latest book or web page. Others will 'show off' in the viva, in an attempt to impress the student, the internal examiner and the supervisor, if the latter is present. This is the 'trumpet blower'. They will spend more time talking about themselves and their own work than the student's. Some will come with, to use the vernacular, a 'set of baggage' or a life story that they carry with them. Others, and fortunately this breed seem to be nearing extinction, seem intent on giving the student a 'hard time' during the viva. It is seen as something to be endured, not enjoyed. Their attitude is reminiscent of the old public school advocates of caning and flogging – 'well, it never did me any harm'. Such examiners present the student with a series of hoops and obstacles to be jumped through, possibly because it gives them a sense of power ('I'll take this student down a peg or two'), or perhaps they may want the student to struggle or suffer a little; but commonly it is a case of 'it happened to me in my viva, so I'll make sure that it happens to you'. This is perhaps more likely to happen when the viva is the external examiner's first. Equally, there may be cases where the internal examiner behaves in some of these strange ways, and the external is perfectly civilised.

An excellent summary of poor practice in oral examinations was given by Partington, Brown and Gordon (1993, 78). They gave labels to certain types, for example:

The inquisitor: this person acts like a hostile TV interviewer, firing questions from the hip, often interrupting and scoring points. This can lead to anger and confrontation as opposed to reasoned discussion. The student is intimidated rather than engaged.

The committee person: the examiner takes the thesis page by page; questioning each point as it arises, thereby avoiding the important, key questions about the contribution of the thesis and its main messages.

The kite flyer: this examiner has a pre-determined view of what the thesis is about and what it is linked to. The examiner explores this link at length, effectively examining a thesis that the student did not write or ever want to write.

The reminiscer: this person bores those present at the viva with stories of his or her own past research and publications, leaving no time for an exploration of the student's work.

THE ORAL EXAMINATION (LIVE VOICE)

The hobbyhorse rider: this examiner is rather like the person above with a bee in the bonnet. They keep coming back to one theme or question, ad nauseam, often with prejudices about certain areas or research studies.

The proofreader: worse than the committee person, the examiner takes the student through the thesis line-by-line, pointing out minor errors and grammatical mistakes.

A university department with strong experience of selecting examiners will usually have good knowledge of whom to avoid and whom to choose. As a result, the viva should be a positive yet demanding experience for a student. The other important decision for a department is to select the right combination of internal and external examiner. There can sometimes be power struggles in this relationship – however, one should not dominate the other; they should be seen as equal partners in the process, whatever their status. Ideally, an external should be chosen who knows the field, will explore all aspects of the thesis fully, will engage the candidate in a fair and demanding discussion but will not intimidate, confront or attempt to impress those present (including the internal).

IMMEDIATELY AFTER THE VIVA: OUTCOMES AND ACTION

Following a viva, most students are asked to wait outside (hopefully, in the supervisor's room rather than a corridor) so that examiners can reach an agreed decision. This may take some time, especially if the examiners cannot immediately reach a consensus. For example, they may need to debate whether the thesis requires minor amendments, more major revisions or should be classed as needing a resubmission. In this process of reaching an agreement, all examiners are of equal worth: no one person should dominate or play the 'I'm a Prof Card'.

When the student comes back to the viva room, and feedback and the decision are given, the supervisor should always be present (even if she/he was not there during the viva). If amendments are asked for, students should take great care to become crystal clear about the points being made and to clarify exactly what they need to do and to write. It is advisable for both parties to take notes and request the examiners put their suggestions for amendment in writing (this should be their duty anyway, according to most regulations). If students seem not to be clear, they should be invited to seek clarification on the action they are being asked to take.

85

JUDGEMENTS, DECISIONS AND THEIR AFTERMATH

A good viva should have covered all the issues raised in the preliminary reports. The viva may contain more if further issues arise during the discussion. A bad viva does not cover all the issues that concern the examiners – this could lead to 'surprise' feedback in the post viva meeting, i.e. feedback which the student (and supervisor if present during the viva) find totally unexpected. Equally, a good viva should have covered all the issues that are then reported back in the post-viva meeting. It would be a bad viva if issues are raised, and amendments are asked for, which are a complete surprise, either to the student or the supervisor who has been a silent observer. Ideally, there should be no surprises after the viva.

Each institution will have some variations in the written regulations, but the outcomes are likely to fall into one of the following categories:

Pass: this is the unusual outcome when a thesis is accepted exactly as it stands, without any need for minor changes or corrections to typos. If the examiners have found absolutely no typographical errors then either yours is the 'cleanest' thesis ever presented or they have not read it word-for-word.

Minor or major amendments: the thesis may be passed, subject to minor amendments. The nature and extent of these can vary – from small alterations, correction of typing errors, or making small revisions to sentences or paragraphs without major changes to the thesis. Examiners may also specify a *small* quantity of additional material to be added, e.g. a strengthening or a more explicit statement of the key messages perhaps. If suggestions for further research are made, this will be classed as either major amendments or referral. There is sometimes a fine line between minor corrections and 'major amendments'. Some universities give a time limit of one month or sometimes six weeks (maximum) for minor changes and indeed some may define the category of 'minor amendments' as those that can realistically be done in a month or six weeks. Often, the changes will need to be approved only by the internal examiner. (See Chapter 8 for more detail.)

Resubmission: again, this can vary enormously from relatively minor amounts of re-writing, e.g. additions or amendments to the concluding chapter, to fairly major requests, such as changing the data analysis and discussion. In one case in our experience, the external even asked the student to go out and collect further data. The maximum time allowed for a resubmission is usually one year.

Students can be asked to resubmit without the need for a further viva, provided the revised thesis is seen and approved by (in most cases) both examiners. In exceptional cases, when the oral has been very unsatisfactory, the recommendation may be for a resubmission followed by another viva.

86

THE ORAL EXAMINATION (LIVE VOICE)

Finally, there may be a requirement for the candidate to undergo another oral examination without modification of the form or content of the written thesis, though this too is unusual.

Fail: this is a very uncommon decision, which should not occur if the thesis has been carefully supervised and the student has taken and followed advice.

Approval for MPhil status: again, this is unlikely in my experience, but it has happened. The doctorate is not awarded but the examiners recommend that the thesis be accepted at Master's level, subject only to necessary changes to the title and cover.

As a final note to the post-viva discussion, an example I have witnessed of not only bad but totally unacceptable practice is for the student to be given a clear statement of her/his amendments and then at a later stage for the examiner checking the amendments to say something of this ilk: 'Well done, but I think you could also make another amendment ... *as follows* ... which would improve your thesis further.' This is not tolerable – a surprise like this for student and supervisor is unacceptable.

VARIATIONS IN VIVAS AND CALLS FOR CHANGE

This chapter has shown that the key variables affecting the nature of a student's oral examination are likely to be:

- The written thesis itself
- The regulations of the awarding university
- The examiners: their views on the thesis; whether they have read and will follow regulations; their 'personal agendas' and the likely 'chemistry' or interpersonal interactions between them and between the student and the examiners.

The first two are relatively clear, at least in the sense that they are written documents, in a way in the public domain. However, the manner in which they have been read and interpreted, alongside the variability in examiners and their personal characteristics, are certainly not clear and are undoubtedly difficult to predict. For those reasons it can be said that every viva is different – however, that is not a logical justification doing away with all vivas.

There has been a range of writing on the 'variations in vivas', their unpredictability and the fact that they are conducted in private. This writing has

JUDGEMENTS, DECISIONS AND THEIR AFTERMATH

raised a number of issues and concerns over the viva as a site of decision making. Perhaps the three main issues reported at that time were:

- The wide variation between vivas, not only between institutions but within them
- The lack of 'transparency' in the conduct of orals
- The lack of 'quality assurance' procedures involved.

Some of those are discussed briefly here, and later I suggest pointers to useful and insightful further reading on this issue. Variability in the conduct and content of vivas has been widely acknowledged (Cryer 2000; Morley et al. 2002; Tinkler and Jackson 2002, and others).

Research from the past showed that there was a lack of clarity and transparency in the conduct and content of the actual viva. This focused on the UK where the oral is conducted behind closed doors, between consenting adults. A couple of decades ago, one author called the viva the 'best kept secret in higher education' (Burnham 1994), while Morley et al. (2002) later talked of variation and 'mystification'. The response in the past to this lack of clarity has been interesting. One extreme suggestion made over two decades ago was to argue for the abolition of the viva: for example Noble (1994, 67) described it as 'an anachronism that can be traced back to the middle ages'. More commonly, there were pleas for the oral to be a public event, similar to the situation in the USA and Scandinavia. Fortunately, neither of these suggestions has been realised.

My own view is that the viva in its current form should be retained. In the past, the viva was subject to very little regulation, accountability and quality assurance, in sharp contrast to other aspects of higher education. Calls were made for transparency, clear guidelines and even nationally agreed standards (Morley et al. 2002); Universities have responded to these calls. The event is no longer a mystery and is subject to 'quality assurance', especially with the advent of the independent Chair. The criticisms of the viva in the past have led, in my view, to hugely improved policy and practice in current doctoral examining.

IN SUMMARY ...

My own experience and research indicates that practice varies across institutions, so written regulations should be examined carefully. The viva is an integral part of a doctoral examination, not an add-on or a rubber-stamping exercise. There are two elements to a doctoral thesis: the written and the

THE ORAL EXAMINATION (LIVE VOICE)

spoken. The viva and the written thesis are important, complementary ways of presenting doctoral work and making them public. The viva should be seen and conducted as a *formative* event, aimed at improving a student's thesis; then its less acknowledged importance becomes clear, i.e. in developing the student's dissertation before it becomes a 'publication' and is housed and catalogued in the university library for others to refer to.

Finally, examiners owe it to students to make the 'live' experience an enjoyable and civilised occasion but at the same time a demanding and possibly mentally exhausting one! I have supervised several students who found their viva a very 'easy' one and who passed with minor corrections but who felt somehow cheated and disappointed by their viva, in the sense that it was not demanding, it did not stretch their thinking and the examiners had not really engaged with their work.

 FURTHER READING

Interesting readings which talk of 'lifting the veil', unravelling the mystery and surviving the viva include:

Burnham, P. 1994. Surviving the Viva: Unravelling the Mysteries of the PhD Oral. *Journal of Graduate Education* 1 (1): 30–34.

Hartley, J., and C. Fox. 2002. The Viva Experience: Examining the Examiners. *Higher Education Review* 35 (1): 24–30.

Hartley, J., and S. Jory. 2000. Lifting the Veil on the Viva: The Experiences of Psychology PhD Candidates in the UK. *Psychology Teaching Review* 9 (2): 76–90.

Morley, L., D. Leonard, and M. David. 2002. Variations in Vivas: Quality and Equality in British PhD Assessments. *Studies in Higher Education* 27 (3): 263–273.

Murray, R. 2003. *How to survive your viva.* Buckingham: Open University Press.

One of the classics on 'behaviour' in vivas which several university regulations still refer to in their guidelines on the oral examination is:

Partington, J., G. Brown, and G. Gordon. 1993. *Handbook for examiners in higher education.* London: CVCP, Staff Development Unit.

For detailed accounts of vivas and what could (and should) be included in the viva voce, see:

Mullins, G., and M. Kiley. 2002. "It's a PhD, Not a Nobel Prize': How Experienced Examiners Assess Research Theses. *Studies in Higher Education* 27 (4): 369–386.

Pearce, L.. 2005. *How to examine a thesis*. Maidenhead: Open University Press.

Tinkler, P., and C. Jackson. 2000. Examining the Doctorate. *Studies in Higher Education* 25: 167–180.

Tinkler, P., and C. Jackson. 2002. In the Dark? Preparing for the PhD Viva. *Quality Assurance in Education* 10 (2): 86–97.

Tinkler, P., and C. Jackson. 2004. *The doctoral examination process: A handbook for students, examiners and supervisors*. Maidenhead: Open University Press.

Trafford, V. 2003. Questions in Doctoral Vivas. *Quality Assurance in Education* 11 (2): 113–121.

Wallace, S. 2002. Figuratively Speaking: Six Accounts of the PhD Viva. *Quality Assurance in Education* 11 (2): 100–108.

WEBSITE

The University of Sheffield has produced an on-line resource for graduate students and staff known as the VGS or Virtual Graduate School, located at:

www.youtube.com/user/vgsschool

One useful video as part of the VGS contains an interview led by Jerry Wellington in which Professor Martin Smith outlines the criteria by which he judges a doctoral thesis and which in turn influence his approach to the viva voce: www.youtube.com/watch?time_continue=136&v=40AHqiDa55o (accessed 18/02/2020)

Chapter 8

Post examination
The examiners' and Chair's roles and responsibilities

THE IMMEDIATE AFTERMATH: ROLES AND RESPONSIBILITIES

The initial decision has been made by the examiners and will be passed on to the 'Research degrees committee' (or similar) to be ratified. The paperwork has been completed, at least partially. The news has been conveyed to the student and supervisor. If a viva has occurred, recommendations will normally have been conveyed orally and time will have been taken to discuss the decision; if necessary, the amendments that the student must make will have been explained face-to-face. If these are minor that may take only a few minutes and time will have been taken to congratulate the student and her supervisor (because this is a good outcome). If amendments are more major and therefore longer and more detailed, time will again be taken to convey these carefully to the student. Whether minor or major, a clear and comprehensive list of the required changes will later need to be put in writing. This is a job for both (or all) of the examiners, together with the Chair.

The key role of the independent, neutral Chair

If an independent Chair has been present, he or she should play a key role in the post-viva discussions. The Chair will probably have been completely quiet for the whole viva but she can join in during the immediate 'aftermath'. The Chair can be a valuable part of the clarification and explaining process. The Chair's role is to:

- See that justice has been done and ensure that the correct regulations have been followed throughout

91

JUDGEMENTS, DECISIONS AND THEIR AFTERMATH

- Be totally clear about the amendments that are required (in a post-viva discussion the supervisor can also join in, mainly to seek clarity)
- Ensure that there are no 'surprises' for either the student or the supervisor(s) (if the latter were present at the viva); the Chair will have read the preliminary reports and the viva should have covered all the issues in those reports. Other issues may have arisen during the viva and these may affect the decision – but the Chair should beware of any shocks or totally unexpected changes or corrections
- Comment on the viva itself and the way it was conducted
- Most difficult of all, the Chair's role is to resolve any disagreements on the decision
- Make sure that the paperwork has been done, including signatures; one of the boxes on the joint report must have been ticked; more detailed paperwork, such as the main body of the examiners' joint report may need to be done by email, with some probable to-ing and fro-ing. The how and who of this must be decided between examiners and the Chair
- Reach agreement on which examiner(s) will check either minor or major amendments.

Finally, the Chair needs to ensure that all the above points are covered before anyone leaves the building prematurely! I have seen this happen, as in 'I must go, I have a train to catch'.

AGREEMENTS AND DISAGREEMENTS

It is unlikely that the examiners will agree on everything. I have seen this happen but it is usually a case of reaching a compromise. Ideally, this should be done face-to-face with the Chair present (if there is one). Quite simply, the examiners have to agree on the decision (i.e. which box to tick!) and eventually on a full statement of the amendments to be made. To state the obvious, they cannot produce two joint reports. The single and signed joint report must contain their joint decision and their joint statement on the thesis, the viva and the amendments necessary. Examiners, in the post-viva meeting, must also agree with all those present on the exact time frame for the required changes.

To stress this point: the joint report must be agreed upon by both or all examiners. It is a joint report. There will always be differences of opinion, especially over the fine detail of the amendments, but disagreements will need to be put aside. This is compromise.

POST EXAMINATION

In a serious case, examiners may have disagreed from the very outset with their preliminary reports; and then they cannot agree on a joint decision or the content of a joint report. I have never experienced this but I have heard of cases where it has happened. Depending on the university's regulations, the only way forward then is to set up a re-examination with two (or more) new examiners. I have been invited to be an examiner after such a situation as this and did agree to do it but was (rightly) never told of the exact circumstances leading up to it.

FEEDING BACK: WRITTEN AS WELL AS SPOKEN

Just a reminder: as we have seen, decisions will depend on the specific regulations of the university holding the examination – so this might vary from minor corrections to major corrections, to resubmission/referral, or in the worst scenario a Fail or recommendation for MPhil. Decisions will be conveyed to the student and supervisor orally if there is a viva; these will be put in writing within a short time frame (I would suggest that, to be fair to the student, a week is a suitable period).

Just to re-emphasise, a face-to-face meeting after a viva will often be an emotional occasion (see later) and adrenaline will be flowing. Hence it is vital that the examiners put together an agreed list of amendments within a reasonable time. This may be possible while the examiners are still in the same room, with the Chair present. However, examiners may need time to reflect on and carefully formulate a clear and comprehensive list of amendments. This list must be provided to the student in writing – hence there is often a need for examiners to 'bat it back and forth' between themselves until they are both completely happy with it.

THE EFFECTS OF THE VIVA ON THE WRITTEN THESIS: GOOD AND BAD VIVAS

A good one...

The oral examination may have gone well: a rich discussion, plenty of challenging questions, a healthy dialogue leading to other, unexpected questions, a good rapport and chemistry between all the participants. This is excellent – enjoyable and satisfying for all, even though it may be exhausting for the student. However, there is a problem with a really good viva. Things arise, questions come up, the student says things and draws conclusions and connections, and even new interpretations of the data may unexpectedly present

93

themselves in a powerful discussion. Perhaps this is inevitable when three or even four good, energetic brains occupy themselves for over an hour with a research project and its findings.

This is excellent but it leads to a complication – valuable things are said in the viva which arise from the student's research work, but which are not stated explicitly, i.e. written down in the submitted dissertation. I have seen this happen many times during a lively, productive, successful viva. They may have come up during the 'conversation' but were simply not there in writing in the thesis; or they may simply not have been made clear enough or given enough emphasis and space. Afterwards, it is the role of the examiners to point this out to student and supervisor. Both of the latter may have realised this during the course of the discussion – this is one of the good reasons for having the supervisor(s) there in the heat of the viva.

The aim of a good viva, as said earlier, is to be formative as well as summative. Its key objective is to make the written thesis a better one before it becomes a publication and enters either a physical library or a virtual one. Thus the role of examiners after a good viva is to point out that the student said certain things (perhaps due the examiners' prompting) which came across really well and/or clearly in the viva but could be improved upon in writing. A good supervisor who has listened throughout may, or perhaps should, also be aware of these pointers to help form an improved thesis. (Incidentally, this happy occurrence always indicates to me the importance of being able to record the viva – though this is rarely permitted by regulations.)

As a result of a good viva, the examiners and chair can agree on the minor amendments that a student must make – as stated elsewhere, these should have arisen during the viva and should not come as a complete surprise to student or supervisor.

Not such a good one...

A less successful viva can, in my experience, be a less enjoyable and sometimes rather tense and tedious affair. A poor viva will show up weaknesses in areas of the student's understanding, such as: their grasp of the literature, their methods and methodology, their analysis of data, their drawing of conclusions and their ability to reflect on and evaluate their own work. The viva may also highlight the student's lack of oral skills. In this case, the role of the examiners is perhaps a tougher one. They will need to act in a formative capacity, to discuss with the student where expansion, or development or criticality is needed. This is perhaps the situation where the examiners really

POST EXAMINATION

earn the small fee that will arrive in their bank account. Their joint report will need to be more detailed and as clear and constructive as possible, without being totally humiliating. This is a hard task and one which requires time to reflect and to compose something (together and perhaps by email) in writing.

This scenario may well lead to a resubmission or a referral and the process will begin again to a large extent. It may also lead to a second viva as we discuss shortly.

ASSESSMENT IS EMOTIONAL

At the risk of sounding un-English (whatever that means), doing a doctorate is emotional. It involves ups and downs, sleepless nights, the occasional euphoric moment but equally plenty of periods of anxiety. The 'journey' or the 'roller coaster' metaphors for doctoral study are clichéd but very apt. The assessment of the doctorate is at least as emotional as the journey leading to it. From the day of submission, the candidate is in something of a state of limbo – wondering how the examiners will react to it, feeling that perhaps they could have done more, and speculating on the choice of examiners and their approach. This anxiety is increased by making a 'live voice' or viva voce into an integral part of the examination. For many students, this will be their first viva. It is to be hoped that they will have presented their work in other fora, such as seminars and conferences. But this will be the first time that two or more people will have read their dissertation in detail (one hopes from cover to cover). It is also the first occasion in which they will have been questioned about its contents, methods and conclusions in great depth over a period of perhaps one or two hours. Assessment is emotional and exhausting.

Hence there is a crucial need for examiners and the Chair (if there is one) to be aware of the student's feelings after the judgement has been made. The candidate's (and the supervisors') emotions may be quite complicated and sometimes (in my experience) surprising. This is covered in an excellent chapter by Tinkler and Jackson (2004, Chapter 13) and their discussion is worth reading in full. My own interpretation of their points, with my own experiences added, is that the candidate's feelings may involve:

- A sense of anti-climax as in 'it's all over, what do I do next?'
- Relief, as in 'it's all over' (similar to the feeling that some gold-medal-winning athletes report)
- It is often not 'all over' so some students will feel disappointment that corrections are required, even if they are minor. They may feel

95

that they have not actually passed and this is why it can be useful for an examiner or the Chair to actually read word for word the box in the joint report that they will be ticking (this will often say 'Pass with minor corrections' for example)

- Students may be delighted but they may feel tired or deflated (this has often surprised me in post-viva feedback sessions)
- They may look somewhat stunned – perhaps their reaction has been delayed or the result has not sunk in
- Some, as in the Connell story from Sally Rooney's book discussed earlier, may feel something of a fraud: do I deserve this? Am I good enough? This imposter syndrome is not uncommon
- In contrast, I have greeted students after a viva who seem to have the unwavering confidence that Connell talks about – as if they expected success all along and the oral examination was just a formality. This has rarely happened but an examiner is likely to find it slightly off-putting and a little annoying!

In summary, the outcomes of doctoral examining will engender a wide range of feelings and emotional reactions. For most of the categories above, the importance of praise and congratulation becomes central. Tinkler and Jackson (2004) stress this when they quote one of the students from their research who was delighted with the praise received from his examiners as he claimed that he 'never received any from his supervisor'.

CHECKING AMENDMENTS: MINOR, LESS MINOR AND RESUBMISSION

It is normally the job of just one of the examiners to check that students make their minor amendments in accordance with the spoken and written instructions given as a result of the joint examiners' report. As stated earlier, these instructions should be crystal clear, totally unambiguous and above all 'do-able'. Thus minor amendments should be do-able within the time limit stated in the university regulations. This limit may be as short as six weeks, though I have seen a three month limit in some cases. If it is humanly impossible for a student to make the required amendments within the stated time frame then they cannot be described as 'minor' on the joint examiners' report. In my view, the time a student needs to make minor amendments can be discussed and even negotiated in the post-viva meeting when everyone (including the supervisor) is present. Thus a part-time doctoral student who has a full-time job (more often the case with a PD student) may need

POST EXAMINATION

longer to complete minor amendments than another student who has just completed a full-time doctorate and does not yet have a job, for example. This is all a matter for civilised discussion as soon as possible after the viva. Generally, I suggest that it is in the student's interest that the maximum time possible should be stated on the joint report, even if in practice the corrections are completed well within this time frame.

As we have seen, if a student is asked to resubmit (with or without a second viva) then both or all examiners will be involved and the entire process (including producing preliminary reports) will start over again, from the beginning.

Procedures for checking amendments

One of the key decisions to be made in filling in the joint report is: who will check that amendments have been made according to the list given to the student? In the case of minor amendments, when the student is not a member of staff, the internal examiner will normally be responsible for checking the amendments with the help of the list provided jointly by the two examiners. When the student is a member of staff, there will be two external examiners – between them, they need to decide who will check the amendments. This decision to take on extra work is sometimes (not always) lubricated by the offer of an additional fee to the chosen one.

How is this checking process usually done? The normal procedure is for the student (with the help of her supervisor) to make the amendments and then to send them to the chosen examiner, usually by email. The onus is on the student to make this as straightforward as possible for the person checking; this can be done by listing the changes made against the original list of corrections asked for and showing exactly where these occur in the written dissertation.

A SECOND VIVA?

One of the decisions that examiners may agree upon is that the student should not now pass but should resubmit their dissertation, and that this must be followed by a second viva. This may, probably will, come as a shock to the student (and perhaps supervisor) so the reasoning behind it must be explained fully to the student, preferably faces to face. Three of the possible reasons for asking for a second viva might be:

- The student's oral skills were not of a standard that satisfied the examiners. In this case, it is vital that examiners and others present at the viva should give full and constructive feedback to the student

JUDGEMENTS, DECISIONS AND THEIR AFTERMATH

after the first viva. How can they prepare, how can they improve and how can they practise their spoken skills?

- The examiners have asked for so many amendments that it will be important to check (during a second viva) that students have made the changes themselves and that they fully understand them.

- I have heard it said that a second viva can also perform the 'ritual'/ occasion function that the first perhaps did not fulfil. It can be an event at which the student is given the opportunity to explain their resubmitted dissertation fully and perhaps to shine. It can then give the examiners an occasion in which they praise the student.

Over a period in which I have examined around one hundred doctoral theses (I haven't counted) I have only been involved in two decisions when a second viva was asked for (incidentally, we all agreed that this decision was the right one). On the first occasion the student had plainly submitted her thesis well before it was ready. It was full of typing errors, unclear sentences and superficial analysis. She was asked to resubmit within a maximum of twelve months and to attend a second viva. Happily, her second submission was far superior and she was able to enjoy her second viva and to explain fully her amendments and her deeper analysis. On the second occasion, the student's first submission was a good one (both examiners agreed) but the student was unable to continue with his viva after we were about twenty minutes into it. He explained that he had been undergoing a lot of personal problems since the work was first submitted and felt that he was not able to do it justice in the face-to-face forum of the first viva. We all agreed that he should be allowed to attend a second viva after a six week period. This was agreed by the relevant committee, the student attended the second viva and was able to explain, clarify, expand, reflect upon and evaluate his work in line with the purposes of a viva outlined in the previous chapter.

IMMEDIATE ADVICE ... OR LONGER TERM SUPPORT PERHAPS?

In some situations students may see you (whether internal or external) as one of the experts in their field – indeed, as we saw earlier, this expertise may be one of the reasons why you were invited to examine. In this case, the student may seek advice and guidance on the development and publication of their work after the doctorate is complete. This can and often is given in the meeting after the viva and in my view this is the collegial thing to do! A few

98

POST EXAMINATION

minutes of discussion and some suggestions for appropriate journals for publishing aspects of the doctorate will be valuable for the student. In other cases I have sometimes seen externals and internals inviting submissions from the student to 'their' journal (if they are the editor) or a journal where they are a member of the editorial board or a referee.

Examiners are under no obligation to offer this oral advice but it is not only civil and collegial, it can also help to promote research and its dissemination in the field of study.

Longer term, students will sometimes ask their examiners for advice (by email for example) in the period well after the examination when they have had the chance to reflect and the adrenaline has eased up. Again, examiners are not obliged to provide advice and guidance and for some it may be seen as 'beyond the call of duty'. My own view is that it is a civil and collegial stance to offer an email response but that this should not be taken too far. I have had students ask me if I would review or comment on a draft paper they had written a few months post-viva, before they send it off to a journal to be subjected to the referees. Personally, I think that this is asking too much of examiners and I would politely refuse and suggest that they should ask their own supervisor or colleagues. I feel that full scale mentoring is not the responsibility of an examiner.

Again longer term, students may wish to involve you in setting up and maintaining a research network; and again, I think this involvement should be at the discretion of the examiners: balancing personal advantage with workload and other demands is the key criterion here.

THE BOOK IN SUMMARY...

Doctoral examining is a unique process in educational assessment. It is of the utmost importance to students and supervisors, not least because it involves a qualification at the highest level. This book has examined the entire doctoral examining process. The book started by tracing the evolution and huge growth of the doctorate over recent decades and how this has influenced its assessment. It continued by examining the meaning of 'doctorateness', exploring the ways in which this is 'played out' in various arenas: written regulations, the doctorate's purpose and impact, the viva voce, and the voices of those involved in the assessment process. Next, the book considered the enactment of doctoral examining in practice by examining the examiners: how do they read a dissertation, what do they look for, who might they be, and how do they interpret the criteria for awarding a

99

doctorate? Subsequent chapters then explored in detail: first, the reports and recommendations that examiners are responsible for completing; and second, the arenas of decision making, including the viva voce (live voice). The viva or oral examination has been explored in full, together with the possible outcomes and the aftermath of the examination process. Finally, the examiners have continuing responsibilities after the initial judgements have been made — these have been considered in detail, both the short term and longer term roles that may be required.

The doctoral examining process is a complex one and is unique in its vital importance, the autonomy afforded to those involved, and the huge input that examiners must make. It is assessment at the highest level. This book has attempted to explore that process in depth, from start to finish. It is intended to be of value to examiners, to students and to supervisors.

 FURTHER READING

For helpful reading on the formative nature of assessment and the ongoing responsibilities of examiners see:

Holbrook, A., S. Bourke, H. Fairbairn, and T. Lovat. 2012. The Focus and Substance of Formative Comment Provided by PhD Examiners. *Studies in Higher Education* 23: 1–18. doi:10.1080/03075079.2012.750289

Jackson, C., and P. Tinkler. 2007. *A guide for internal and external examiners*. London: Society for Research into Higher Education.

Tinkler, P., and C. Jackson. 2004. *The doctoral examination process: A handbook for students, examiners and supervisors*. Maidenhead: SRHE and Open University Press.

From a student's perspective, especially the viva and publication post-viva, see:

Wellington, J. 2003. *Getting published*. London: Routledge.

Wellington, J., A. Bathmaker, C. Hunt, G. McCulloch, and P. Sikes. 2005. *Succeeding with your doctorate*. London: Sage.

References

Bourdon, R. 1974. *Education, opportunity and social inequality*. New York: Wiley.

Bourke, S. 2007. PhD Thesis Quality. *South African Journal of Higher Education* 21 (8): 1042–1052.

Bourke, S., J. Hattie, and L. Anderson. 2004. Predicting Examiner Recommendations on PhD Theses. *International Journal of Educational Research* 41 (2): 178–194.

Bourke, S., and A. Holbrook. 2013. Examining PhD and Research Masters Theses. *Assessment & Evaluation in Higher Education* 38 (4): 407–416.

Burnham, P. 1994. Surviving the Viva: Unravelling the Mysteries of the PhD Oral. *Journal of Graduate Education* 1 (1): 30–34.

Carter, S. 2008. Examining the Doctoral Thesis. *Innovations in Education and Teaching International* 45 (4): 365–374.

Cryer, P. 2000. *The research student's guide to success*. Buckingham: Open University Press.

Delamont, S., P. Atkinson, and O. Parry. 2000. *The doctoral experience: Success and failure in graduate school*. London: Falmer Press.

Denicolo, P. 2003a. Assessing the PhD. *Quality Assurance in Education* 11 (2): 84–91.

Denicolo, P. 2003b. Assessing the Ph.D.: A Constructive View of Criteria for Research Degree Examining. *Quality in Education* 11 (2): 84–91.

Denicolo, P., and C. Park. 2010. *Doctorateness an elusive concept?* Gloucester: The Quality Assurance Agency for Higher Education.

Devos, A., and M. Somerville. 2012. What Constitutes Doctoral Knowledge? *Australian Universities Review* 54 (1): 47–55.

Economic and Social Research Council. 2005. *Postgraduate training guidelines*. Swindon: ESRC.

Gallie, W. B. 1956. Essentially Contested Concepts. *Proceedings of the Aristotelian Society* 56: 167–198.

Golding, C., S. Sharmini, and A. Lazarovitch. 2014. What Examiners Actually Do: What Thesis Students Should Know. *Assessment & Evaluation in Higher Education* 39 (5): 563–576.

Grabbe, L. 2003. The Trials of Being a PhD External Examiner. *Quality Assurance in Education* 11 (2): 128–133.

REFERENCES

Green, H., and S. Powell. 2005. *Doctoral study in contemporary higher education.* Buckingham: Open University Press.

Hartley, J., and L. Betts. 2009. Publishing before the Thesis. *Higher Education Review* 41 (3): 29–44.

Hartley, J., and C. Fox. 2002. The Viva Experience: Examining the Examiners. *Higher Education Review* 35 (1): 24–30.

Hartley, J., and S. Jory. 2000. Lifting the Veil on the Viva: The Experiences of Psychology PhD Candidates in the UK. *Psychology Teaching Review* 9 (2): 76–90.

Hockey, J. 1997. A Complex Craft: UK PhD Supervision in the Social Sciences. *Research in Post-Compulsory Education* 2 (1): 45–70.

Jackson, C., and P. Tinkler. 2001. Back to Basics: A Consideration of the Purposes of the PhD. *Assessment & Evaluation in Higher Education* 26 (4): 355–366.

Jackson, C., and P. Tinkler. 2007. *A guide for internal and external examiners.* London: Society for Research into Higher Education.

Lee, A., and B. Kamler. 2008. Bringing Pedagogy to Doctoral Publishing. *Teaching in Higher Education* 13: 511–523.

Leonard, D., R. Becker, and K. Coate. 2005. To Prove Myself at the Highest Level: The Benefits of Doctoral Study. *Higher Education Research & Development* 24 (2): 135–149.

Maxwell, T. W., T. Evans, and C. Hickey. 2004. Professional Doctorates : Working Towards Impact, in Professional Doctorates : The Impact of Professional Doctorates in the Workplace and Professions. Proceedings of the 5th Professional Doctorates Conference, 2004, Research Institute for Professional & Vocational Education & Training, Deakin University, Geelong, Vic., pp. 1–7, http://hdl.handle.net/10536/DRO/DU:30025749

Morley, L. 2004. Interrogating Doctoral Assessment. *International Journal of Educational Research* 41 (2): 1–97.

Morley, L., D. Leonard, and M. David. 2002. Variations in Vivas: Quality and Equality in British PhD Assessments. *Studies in Higher Education* 27 (3): 263–273.

Mullins, G., and M. Kiley. 2002. 'It's a PhD, Not a Nobel Prize': How Experienced Examiners Assess Research Theses. *Studies in Higher Education* 27 (4): 369–386.

Neumann, D. 2007. Policy and Practice in Doctoral Education. *Studies in Higher Education* 32 (4): 459–473.

Neumann, R. 2003. *The doctoral education experience: Diversity and complexity.* Canberra: Australian Government, Department of Education, Science and Training.

Neumann, R. 2005. Doctoral Differences: Professional Doctorates and PhDs Compared. *Journal of Higher Education Policy and Management* 27 (2): 173–188.

Noble, K. A. 1994. *Changing doctoral degrees: An international perspective.* Buckingham: Society for Research into Higher Education and Open University Press.

Park, C. 2005. New Variant PhD: The Changing Nature of the Doctorate in the UK. *Journal of Higher Education Policy and Management* 27 (2): 189–207.

Park, C. 2007. *Redefining the doctorate.* York: Higher Education Academy.

Phillips, E., and D. Pugh. 2015. *How to get a PhD.* Maidenhead: Open University Press.

Popper, K. 1968. *The logic of scientific discovery.* London: Routledge.

102

REFERENCES

Powell, S., and H. Green. 2007. *The doctorate worldwide*. Buckingham: Open University Press.

Quality Assurance Agency for Higher Education (QAA). 2004. *Code of practice for the assurance of academic quality and standards in higher education*. Gloucester: QAA.

QAA. 2015. Characteristics Statement: Doctoral Degree. Gloucester: QAA. www.qaa.ac.uk/docs/qaa/quality-code/doctoral-degree-characteristics-15.pdf?sfvrsn=50aef981_10

Roberts, G. 2002. *SET for success: Final report of Sir Gareth Roberts' review*. London: HM Treasury.

Rooney, S. 2018. *Normal people*. London: Faber and Faber.

Scott, D., A. Brown, I. Lunt, and L. Thorne. 2004. *Professional doctorates: Integrating professional and academic knowledge*. Maidenhead: Open University Press.

Shaw, M., and H. Green. 2002. Benchmarking the PhD: A Tentative Beginning. *Quality Assurance in Education* 10 (2): 116–124.

Simpson, R. 1983. *How the PhD came to Britain*. Guildford: Society for Research into Higher Education.

Taylor, S., and N. Beasley. 2005. *A handbook for doctoral supervisors*. London: Routledge Falmer.

Tinkler, P., and C. Jackson. 2000. Examining the Doctorate. *Studies in Higher Education* 25: 167–180.

Tinkler, P., and C. Jackson. 2004. *The doctoral examination process: A handbook for students, examiners and supervisors*. Maidenhead: Open University Press.

Trafford, V. 2003. Questions in Doctoral Vivas. *Quality Assurance in Education* 11 (2): 113–121.

United Kingdom Council for Graduate Education. 2002. *Professional doctorates*. Lichfield: UKCGE.

Usher, R. 2002. A Diversity of Doctorates: Fitness for the Knowledge Economy? *Higher Education Research and Development* 21 (2): 143–153.

Wallace, S. 2002. Figuratively Speaking: Six Accounts of the PhD Viva. *Quality Assurance in Education* 11 (2): 100–108.

Wellington, J. 2003. *Getting published*. London: Routledge.

Wellington, J. 2010a. *Making supervision work for you*. London: Sage.

Wellington, J. 2010b. Supporting Students' Preparation for the Viva: Their Preconceptions and Implications for Practice. *Teaching in Higher Education* 15 (2): 135–150.

Wellington, J. 2013. Searching for Doctorateness. *Studies in Higher Education* 38 (10): 1490–1503.

Wellington, J., A. M. Bathmaker, C. Hunt, G. McCulloch, and P. Sikes. 2005. *Succeeding with your doctorate*. London: Sage Publications Ltd.

Wellington, J., and P. Sikes. 2006. A Doctorate in a Tight Compartment: Why Do Students Choose A Professional Doctorate and What Impact Does It Have on Their Personal and Professional Lives? *Studies in Higher Education* 31 (6): 723–734.

Wellington, J. and M. Szczerbinski. 2008. *Research methods for the social sciences*. London: Continuum.

REFERENCES

Winter, R., M. Griffith, and K. Green. 2000. The Academic Qualities of Practice. *Studies in Higher Education* 25 (1): 25–37.

Wittgenstein, L. 1968. *Philosophical investigations*. Cambridge: Cambridge University Press.

Wittgenstein, L. 1981. *Tractatus logico-philosophicus*. Ed. D.F. Pears. London: Routledge.

Yang, R. 2012. Up and Coming? Doctoral Education in China. *Australian Universities Review* 54 (1): 64–69.

Index

abstracts 46–7
amendments 65–9, 96–100
asking questions (in a viva) 80–3
assessment 3–100
'audit culture' 3–5, 15

'bad practice' 83–5
being critical 54–6, 60, 63
benefits of examining 14–15, 47–8

Chair (neutral, independent) 14, 45, 53, 56, 75–6, 79, 88, 91–5
choosing examiners 41–4
chronology (of the exam process) 41–3
context (for the doctorate) 3–17
criteria (for doctorates) 24–6, 31–8, 63, 71–2
criticality 54–6, 60, 63
critique 54–6, 60, 63

diversity (of doctorates) 4–9, 16, 18–19
doctoral titles 7
'doctorateness' 18–29, 30–8

emotional aspects (of exams) 19, 70, 74, 93, 95–6
examination process 30–100
examiners ('good' and 'bad') 41–4
external examiners 41–4, 64–5

feedback 93–5

formative assessment 6, 52, 59–60, 66, 89, 100
frameworks (for doctorates) 41–2

generic skills 3–5
global perspectives 12–14, 44–5
'good' examiners 41–4, 82–3
'good' theses 48–50

idioms 83
impact 4, 6, 22–4, 28–9
independent Chair 14, 45, 53, 56, 75–6, 79, 88, 91–5
independent reports 51–60
internal examiners 48, 64–5, 75, 77, 84–5, 100

knowledge, modes of 11–12

literature review 14–15, 32, 47, 49, 54–6, 59, 66, 80, 94

major amendments 65–9, 96–100
managing time (as an examiner) 47–8
minor amendments 65–9, 96–100
modes of knowledge 11–12
modes of submission 7–8
motivation 20–2

neutral Chair 14, 45, 53, 56, 75–6, 79, 88, 91–5

105

INDEX

oral examinations 31–3, 56–7, 66, 69, 71–90
originality 24–7, 35–6, 64
outcomes (of examination) 65–70, 85–100

parity of esteem 8–9
perspectives (on the exam process) 33–63, 73–4, 100
PhD by publication 7–9
post examination 68–9, 91–100
preliminary reports 51–60
practice-based doctorates 13, 17, 19, 52, 60
process and product 22–3, 53–4
professional doctorates (PD, prof doc) 8, 16, 23–4, 34, 43–7, 57
public vivas 72–3
'publishability' 25, 58, 64, 80
purposes (of the doctorate) 20–22

quality control 3–5
questioning (good and bad) 80–3

reading the thesis 45–7
Recommendations 65–70

regulations 3–5
resubmission/referral 65–9, 79, 85–6, 93–6
Roberts Review 3–5
routes to the doctorate 7–9

second viva 97–8
students' perspectives 33–6, 73–4, 100
supervision 3–6, 9–10, 12, 15, 22, 34, 54

theory 26–7, 32
theses (good and bad) 48–51
transferable skills 3–5
types of doctorate 7–9

variability (in examining) 30, 63, 87–90
variations in vivas 87–90
viva voce 31–3, 56–7, 66, 69, 71–90

ways of being original 24–7, 35–6, 64
written criteria 24–6, 31–8, 63, 71–2
written regulations 24–6, 31–8, 63, 71–2

106